Shakespeare's Comedies: A Very Short Introduction

VERY SHORT INTRODUCTIONS are for anyone wanting a stimulating and accessible way into a new subject. They are written by experts, and have been translated into more than 40 different languages.

The Series began in 1995, and now covers a wide variety of topics in every discipline. The VSI library now contains over 450 volumes—a Very Short Introduction to everything from Psychology and Philosophy of Science to American History and Relativity—and continues to grow in every subject area.

Very Short Introductions available now:

Available soon:

THE WELFARE STATE David Garland

CRYSTALLOGRAPHY A. M. Glazer

ASTROPHYSICS James Binney

AGRICULTURE Paul Brassley and Richard Soffe

ISOTOPES Rob Ellam

For more information visit our website

www.oup.com/vsi/

Bart van Es

SHAKESPEARE'S COMEDIES

A Very Short Introduction

OXFORD
UNIVERSITY PRESS

Great Clarendon Street, Oxford, OX2 6DP,
United Kingdom

Oxford University Press is a department of the University of Oxford.
It furthers the University's objective of excellence in research, scholarship,
and education by publishing worldwide. Oxford is a registered trade mark of
Oxford University Press in the UK and in certain other countries

Published in the United States of America by Oxford University Press
198 Madison Avenue, New York, NY 10016, United States of America

British Library Cataloguing in Publication Data
Data available

Library of Congress Control Number: 2015955586

ISBN 978-0-19-872335-6

Printed and bound by
CPI Group (UK) Ltd, Croydon, CR0 4YY

Contents

List of illustrations

Chronology

Shakespeare's Comedies

Introduction

What is a Shakespearean comedy?

The following plays are listed under 'Comedies' in the 1623 Folio edition of Shakespeare's works:

The Tempest (1611)
The Two Gentlemen of Verona (1590–1)
The Merry Wives of Windsor (1597–8)
Measure for Measure (1603)
The Comedy of Errors (1594)
Much Ado About Nothing (1598)
Love's Labour's Lost (1594–5)
A Midsummer Night's Dream (1595)
The Merchant of Venice (1596–7)
As You Like It (1600)
The Taming of the Shrew (1590–1)
All's Well that Ends Well (1604–5)
Twelfth Night (1601)
The Winter's Tale (1609–10)

The list is obviously not in chronological order and the dates of composition added in brackets, based on the current scholarly consensus, are my addition to the original text. To these fourteen plays we could possibly add *Pericles* (composed in

1607 but excluded from the Folio) and *The Two Noble Kinsmen* (a romance of 1613–14 co-authored with John Fletcher that was not published until 1634). There is also a case to be made for the inclusion of *Troilus and Cressida* (1602), which is described as a witty comedy in the preface to one of the 1609 Quartos (although the Folio editors initially planned to include it in the list of Shakespeare's tragedies and then squeezed it in as the last of the 'Histories' when they had trouble with the text). Even *Cymbeline* (1610), which was somewhat oddly listed as Tragedy, could be added given that there is not much to separate it from *The Winter's Tale* in terms of subject matter, plot, or style. Finally, one could add *Cardenio* (1612–13), a lost play that some scholars feel left its mark on a much later work, *Double Falsehood*, which came with debatable claims of Shakespearean authorship. At a generous count, then, very nearly half of Shakespeare's plays can be described as comedies of some kind.

The author of *a Very Short Introduction* could get even greedier by pointing out that several of the histories and tragedies contain a high proportion of comic material (Hamlet is a great joker, *Lear* (1605–6) includes the Fool's role, and Falstaff of the *Henry IV* plays (1596–8) is possibly the greatest comic creation in the canon).

On the other hand, it is possible to apply more restrictive criteria. *The Tempest* (1611) and *The Winter's Tale* (1609–10) can be described instead as 'romances' or 'tragi-comedies' and the same could be said for *Pericles* (1607), *Two Noble Kinsmen* (1613–14), and *Troilus and Cressida* (1602). According to this classification the comedies would amount to less than third of Shakespeare's total output. Going still further, some critics have called *Measure for Measure* (1603), *All's Well That Ends Well* (1604–5), and even *The Merchant of Venice* (1596–7) 'problem plays' rather than comedies. *The Taming of the Shrew* (1590–1) (whose main plot centres on a man who bullies his wife into submission) is likewise problematic for modern audiences as a comedy and *The Two Gentlemen of Verona* concludes with its heroine being married to a man who, minutes before, has attempted the rape of her friend. Whittling away in this manner it is possible to end up with just half a dozen true, festive Shakespearean comedies.

Lists and attempts at definition are inevitably problematic, which is the first thing that a Short Introduction must acknowledge. Still, as with other troublesome categories (such as 'art' or 'pornography'), there is a sense that we know a Shakespearean comedy when we see it. This book sets out to isolate that quality, to show why the plays are special, and also to compare Shakespeare's work in this genre to that of his contemporaries and to place it within the history and theory of comedy across time. There is always the danger that analysis will kill comedy, but I will do my best to give perspectives that make the plays more interesting and even (ideally) more fun.

Comedy before Shakespeare

Before setting out what is distinctive to Shakespeare's own contribution it is useful, briefly, to look at the kind of comedy he would have encountered before he himself started to write. As with most things, his first contact must have come in Stratford, where, like all grammar school pupils, he would have studied the Latin comedies of Plautus and Terence. Quite possibly, as part of his education, he would have performed in them as well. Though varied, these plays tend to centre on a limited set of stock characters: wily slaves, ambitious young men in search of love, rich merchant fathers, and attractive courtesans. Their action plays out in public space in front of a set of fixed 'houses' and it builds gradually in its level of confusion until the 'catastrophe' brings resolution to the various strands of the plot. In the end, the young men tend to get what they desire, their fathers are defeated, and hidden identities are revealed.

As well as the plays themselves, Shakespeare would have picked up something of Donatus's famous generalizations about them, which became, in the 16th century, a basic rulebook for the differences between comedy and tragedy:

> Of the many differences between tragedy and comedy, the foremost are these: in comedy the fortunes of men are middle-class, the dangers are slight, and the ends of the action are happy; but in tragedy everything is the opposite—the characters are great men, the fears are intense, and the ends disastrous. In comedy the beginning is troubled, the end tranquil; in tragedy events follow the reverse order. And in tragedy the kind of life is shown that is to be shunned; while in comedy the kind is shown that is to be sought after. Finally in comedy the story is always fictitious; while tragedy often has a basis in historical truth.

Decorum (fitting the right kind of speech to the social level of the characters) was important to the schoolmasters who taught these comedies, as was the correct ordering and unity of action in their plots. Not only old plays, but also many new ones were written in accordance with this formula. Italian plays composed on the classical model were especially admired: these were available in the original but also translated into English, often in an adapted form. George Gascoigne's *Supposes* (1566), which eventually influenced Shakespeare's *The Taming of the Shrew* (1590–1) and *The Comedy of Errors* (1594), is an example of such an adapted Italian-Classical play. In schools, universities, and at court, such erudite dramas, composed roughly in accordance with the rules of so-called New Comedy, were hard to avoid.

This, though, was not the only comic tradition that Shakespeare would have encountered. There was also the native drama of morality plays and interludes, with its origins in the middle ages, which was still widely performed at court and also by troupes of travelling players throughout the land. This kind of work was much more of a hotchpotch, mixing knockabout clowning and dancing with serious moral instruction. In its earliest versions it featured a kind of trickster, known as the Vice, who liked to deliver wisecracks directly to the audience and whose object was to mislead the central character, who was often a kind of everyman. Plays as diverse as the serious biblical morality *The Life and Repentance of Mary Magdalen* (1550) and the English street farce *Jack Juggler* (1555) contain a Vice who is a spokesperson for chaos and self-indulgence and thus also for comedy as a principle in life.

When Shakespeare came to settle in London at some point in the late 1580s or very early 1590s he would have encountered a vibrant culture of commercial public theatre that drew on these two traditions: on the one hand, the classical tradition of the grammar schools, and, on the other, the less structured jesting and clowning that grew from the morality play. A work like John Lyly's *Mother Bombie* (1589), first performed by a company of boy actors, is an example from the classical side of the spectrum: it is set in England but most of the characters have classical names and the plot, which involves a set of fathers who wish to block their offspring's marriage, runs neatly from confused identities at the beginning to reconciliation at the end. *A Knack to Know a Knave* (1592), which involved the 'applauded merriments' of Will Kemp (the future star comedian of Shakespeare's acting company, see Figure 1), is much closer to an old morality: it has allegorical characters such as 'Honesty' mixed in with historical figures and has an episodic structure that brings various kinds of misdemeanour to light. Both these plays (and many more in the vast range of compositions that lay between them) could be called comedies. They drew audiences in their thousands, not just in the indoor and outdoor play spaces of London but also at court and on provincial tours. There was thus a ready market for anyone who could pen a good play.

1. **Will Kemp, detail from _Nine Days Wonder_ (1600).**

The market for comedy in Shakespeare's time

It is not easy to date Shakespeare's plays but according to the
conventional chronology his first solo effort was a comedy: _The
Two Gentlemen of Verona_, completed between 1590 and 1591.
This story of the lust-transformed Proteus and his true love
Julia (who follows him disguised as a boy), is strongly
influenced by the plays of John Lyly. At the same time, the
set routines involving Lance the clown and his dog Crab
have much in common with the 'applauded merriments' of

A Knack to Know a Knave. Like many of his contemporaries, Shakespeare thus pitched his plays to the middle of the market, appealing both to an elite audience and to the mass of spectators who attended the public stage.

At the time he wrote *The Two Gentlemen of Verona* Shakespeare was starting out as a freelance author, selling his work to rival troupes of actors who were performing in London. *The Taming of the Shrew* written a year or so later, for example, seems to have been sold to the Earl of Pembroke's Men. In 1594, however, Shakespeare became a shareholder in a newly formed acting company, the Lord Chamberlain's Men, and from that point onwards he wrote only for this specific group. Roughly speaking, for the next decade he kept up a pattern of writing one comedy and one serious play each year. Once written, the plays stayed in the company's repertory so that, for example, *Love's Labour's Lost* (1594–5) could still be called up at the last minute for a court performance before a new monarch in 1605.

As with everything else, there were changing fashions in comedy. At the turn of the century, for example, there was a fad for so-called 'humours' comedy, based on characters with extreme singular traits. George Chapman's *An Humorous Day's Mirth* (1597) is one of the earliest examples. It features the melancholic Dowsecer (an absurd depressive), the repetitive Blanvel (who irritatingly echoes whatever is said to him), and the puritanical Countess Florila (revealed, ultimately, as a hypocrite). The children's acting companies, which reopened their doors in 1600 after a decade of closure, added to the diversity of provision. These outfits of boy players, performing at more expensive indoor playhouses, specialized in satire. Ben Jonson wrote *Poetaster* (1601–2) for them, which mocked rival playwrights John Marston and Thomas Dekker, who then responded in kind with their own satirical play.

Shakespeare, in part because of his special status as company shareholder, stayed above such personal rivalry and did not write either humoural or satirical plays. Clearly, though, he was influenced by the work of his contemporaries. John Marston's innovation of tragicomedy in *The Malcontent* (1603), for example, greatly interested Shakespeare—so much so that he and his fellows in the company had the play adapted from its original child actor version for performance by the adults at the Globe. Marston's darkly comic picture of court corruption had an immediate impact on Shakespeare's own writing and must be counted as a contributing factor to the very different tone of Shakespeare's 'problem comedies' at this time. At a later stage too, the children had a transformative effect on the playwright's comedy, with John Fletcher's pastoral tragicomedies, such as *The Faithful Shepherdess* (1607), bringing a new quality of magical wonder to Shakespeare's comic work. Indeed, in his final years, Shakespeare preferred to write in collaboration with Fletcher, producing plays that were designed for performance on both the outdoor and the indoor stage.

By the end of Shakespeare's career in 1614 the market for plays was significantly different to what it had been when he started out nearly a quarter of a century earlier. Clowns and jigs, so long central to the popular tradition, were now widely mocked (even if they were not entirely excluded from the repertory). Playwriting had become a more socially elevated profession: most authors were now university men from educated families (instead of being, like Shakespeare and many others of his generation, the grammar-school-educated sons of artisans). Indoor theatres had become much more important while the open air amphitheatres, like the Globe, were starting to lose their allure for the gentleman class. In this climate literary comedy was becoming more urbane and rakish and Shakespeare's last compositions, the lost *Cardenio* (1612–13) and *The Two Noble Kinsmen* (1613–14) (both co-authored), reflect that fact. Yet, in spite of developing fashions, the earlier comedies continued their popularity, still appearing on the stage (sometimes in lightly revised versions) and also (in the case of *Taming of the Shrew*, *The Merchant of Venice*, and *Love's Labour's Lost*) appearing in print. Shakespeare, as Ben Jonson put it in his prefatory poem for the 1623 Folio, was 'not of an age, but for all time'.

The comedies after Shakespeare

The trends that were in evidence in the final years of Shakespeare's career continued into and beyond the middle of the century. The year 1642 saw the outbreak of the Civil War and the closure of the theatres, which, at the Restoration in 1660, returned in a more expensive, indoor version, with female actors and sliding backdrop scenery. Restoration theatre was strongly focused on the attractiveness of its actresses and so, unsurprisingly, Shakespeare's comedies were cut and altered to increase their sex appeal. An early success, for example, was William Davenant's *The Law Against Lovers* (1662), which fused the Beatrice and Benedick plot from *Much Ado About Nothing* (1598) with the plot of *Measure for Measure* (1603), thus producing a more upbeat comedy that also satirized the dark days of the Commonwealth in the form of Angelo's puritan reign.

The Law Against Lovers shows how Shakespeare's plays were changed after his death in three related areas: the depiction of women; the treatment of politics; and the variation of theatrical design. The Restoration, with its cult of the rake and its innovation of female acting, promulgated a more aggressive, voyeuristic sexuality. William Wycherley's *The Plain Dealer* (1676), very loosely based on *Twelfth Night*, provides an extreme example: the Viola figure (Fidelia) is actually stripped of her male disguise in front of the audience and nearly raped. These things had changed very markedly by the time we get to David Garrick's mid-18th-century productions, which were more faithful to Shakespeare's text but also more determined to 'promote decency and inspire virtue' in the way they presented comedy on the stage.

Unlike the actor-managers of the Restoration era, Garrick and his successors were reluctant to alter Shakespeare's language, in part because they had a much deeper sense of veneration for the playwright as a genius set apart from ordinary men. The respect they had for the Shakespeare's morality and sensibility, however, also made them determined to eliminate the aspects of the comedies that were likely to cause offence. Garrick's 1754 adaptation of *The Taming of the Shrew* (1590–1), entitled *Catharine and Petruchio*, is the most striking instance of this practice. This production entirely cut the original 'Induction', which makes the story of Kate and Petruchio itself a theatrical performance that is put on by a group of players in front of the drunken tinker Christopher Sly. The 18th-century version, with its lavish scenery, was much more dignified in its visual presentation. More importantly, however, Garrick changed the characters (while almost entirely preserving Shakespeare's dialogue), removing Petruchio's violence and giving hints that Catherine loves him early on. His Petruchio (played by Henry Woodward, see Figure 2) was a perfect gentleman, whose 'antic disposition' (used to tame Catherine) existed only 'for the nonce'. In terms of plot, only Shakespeare's notorious end on Katherina's 'submission' needed changing: her speech on the proper position of women was now directed at her sister, prompted not by a wager but by a 'well placed' feminine faith in her husband's virtuous intent. Other parts of her speech were put into the mouth of Petruchio, recast as sensible masculine advice. Whether these changes actually made Shakespeare's play less sexist is questionable, but they did make it more conventionally romantic and genteel.

Victorian productions carried things much further in this direction, both in terms of gentility and as regards lavishness of set design. The realism and sentimentality of the 19th-century novel made its way into stage production, so that, for example, Charles Kean's 1856 *A Midsummer Night's Dream* placed the Acropolis on the Athenian skyline and even depicted authentic Greek carpentry as an occupation for the rude mechanicals.

Shakespeare's Comedies

2. Benjamin van der Gucht, 'Henry Woodward as Petruchio in Garrick's *Catharine and Petruchio* (1756), Yale Center for British Art.

Shakespearean comedy on the Victorian stage was an immersive experience, with theatrical actor-managers such as Henry Irving setting out to transport their audiences in place and time. Irving, as manager of the London Lyceum, established the practice of darkening the auditorium (so that the audience saw only the stage and not each other) and used gaslight with filters to create breath taking light effects upon the stage. His 1882 *Much Ado About Nothing*, starring Ellen Terry as a beautiful, sprightly, feminine, warm-hearted Beatrice (see Figure 3), was the apotheosis of the period's glamorous and wholesome perspective on Shakespeare's comedies. Everything about the production was resplendent, sparing neither time nor expense: the cathedral set for Hero and Claudio's wedding took fifteen minutes to build on stage.

The conservatism of Irving's perspective on Shakespeare's comedy ran deep. Distinctions between male and female were reassuringly absolute; social issues (such as prostitution or political corruption) were repressed; and—at a more conceptual level—the world on stage remained separate from the audience, almost as much as if they had been watching film. This vision of Shakespearean comedy still has a hold on our collective imagination, even if we do not attribute it directly to the 19th-century stage. Until very recently, for example, printed editions of the plays still liked to begin individual scenes by describing a 'location', thus giving a fixity to stage space that was much more Victorian than Elizabethan in its origin. So too, editions began with lists of *dramatis personae*, ranking first the male characters in order of prominence and then the women. Based on such absolute stratification, modern audiences and readers often still make confident pronouncements about 'society's attitude to women' in Shakespeare's era, invoking an idea of 'stage realism' or 'femininity' that has much more to do with Victorian assumptions than it has with Shakespeare's own.

Post-Victorian interpretations of Shakespeare, both by stage professionals and by critics, have often worked to explode such assumptions about the stability of the playwright's ethos. These dramatic productions and critical readings have revealed a more contentious aspect to the comedies, especially as regards gender, sexuality, race, and class. The 20th century saw the advent of

MISS ELLEN TERRY AS "BEATRICE."

COPYRIGHT.

WINDOW & GROVE   63ᴬ BAKER STREET, W.

3. Ellen Terry as Beatrice at the Lyceum (1882).

directorial Shakespeare: the modern convention of a specific production involving set design, costume, and a particular cast of actors that is unified by a director's vision of the play as a whole. While actor managers like Garrick or Irving in earlier centuries certainly had control over their theatres, they were much less self-conscious about offering an *interpretation* when they put on a play. This changed in the new era, with radical thinkers such as Harley Granville-Barker determined to challenge all of the old assumptions of the commercial stage. Granville-Barker stripped away Victorian realism and restored much of the text that was conventionally cut in 19th-century productions. Influenced by the socialist playwright George Bernard Shaw, he recovered some of the edgy, expressive power of Shakespeare's comedy, thereby anticipating what later directors would achieve.

Granville-Barker's 1912 production of *A Midsummer Night's Dream* at the Savoy Theatre was a radical move away from the chocolate-box productions (in one case featuring real rabbits) that had pleased the crowds a generation earlier. Instead of pretty children, his fairies were inhuman and sinister, dressed all in gold and moving with choreographed regularity through an abstract forest of purple and green. This was a much more elite, intellectual way of thinking about Shakespeare, closely connected to modernist art. When the subsidized National Theatre for which Granville-Barker campaigned eventually came into being it would be characterized by sophisticated high-concept productions such as his.

As a director and also as a critic through his *Prefaces to Shakespeare*, Granville-Barker was extremely influential. He understood the plays as having a kind of symphonic coherence (consisting of symbols, themes, and characters in structural conflict); in the words of John Gielgud 'he was like a wonderful conductor of an orchestra'. For the comedies, this musical approach was especially important. In his advice on staging the unfashionable, highly stylized play *Love's Labour's Lost* (1594–5), for example, Granville-Barker wrote about the work's 'rhythm', not just in its rhetoric but in the to and fro between the characters themselves. On the stage characters like constable Dull and the clown Costard had to stand as counterpoint to the aristocrats and this was to be reflected in the colour scheme of a production. It is as follows, for example, that Granville-Barker set out 'the pictorial values in the pageantry' of the final aborted wooing scene:

> Yesterday Navarre and his friends were recluse philosophers; splendid even so, no doubt, but with a pallid spendour. To-day they are in love and glowingly apparelled, in which symbolism their ladies can match them; and against this delicately blended colouring the village pageant tells crude and loud. Into the midst there suddenly steps Marcade, in black from head to foot.

Even if this description sounds a little hammy to modern readers, the directorial approach taken by Granville-Barker is now standard for the way Shakespeare's comedies appear on stage. Today's audiences expect a coherent picture, which is often expressed by setting the play at a particular historical point in time. The Royal Shakespeare Company (RSC)'s 2014 *Love's Labour's Lost*, for example, set the story in an English country house just before World War I. Such directorial decisions, like those of literary critics, involve deliberate polemic (in this case stressing the horrors of war). Productions of the comedies can be feminist, anti-capitalist, or can draw attention to imperialist or racist politics that might lie hidden in a play. A staging of *The Merchant of Venice* now inevitably confronts anti-Semitism, while *The Tempest* is often cast in a manner that makes Prospero (as the new ruler of Caliban's island) a colonial master whose absolute power is far from straightforwardly just. Most conspicuously, performances of *The Taming of the Shrew* were changed by the women's movement that took shape in the 1970s, so that the play's ending on Katherine's submission (which, even in Shakespeare's day was considered problematic) could no longer be softened (as it had been in productions since Garrick's) into something mutually beneficial for man and wife. Coloured by the feminist movement,

Michael Bogdanov's 1978 RSC version, starring Paola Dionisotti, thus depicted the play's conclusion as a tragedy, with Katherine walking off stage as a broken woman, just as if she were Nora Helmer in Ibsen's *A Doll's House*.

If there ever was a consistent idea of what 'Shakespearean comedy' consists of that idea has now vanished. On the stage, a play like *Measure for Measure* (1603) can now exist in radically different versions: on the one hand in productions that aim for historical authenticity, such as those in reconstructed original playhouses like the Sam Wanamaker or Shakespeare's Globe; on the other, in daring reinventions, such as Cheek by Jowl's 2015 Russian translation, which parallels the play to President Putin's elected dictatorship. Academic debate highlights gender politics (including androgyny and transsexual representation), nationalism, green issues, and even the ethics of child acting on Shakespeare's stage. In this context producing *a Very Short Introduction* is an exciting but daunting prospect. What coherent analysis is possible when every trend is towards multiples, polarities, and subdivisions?

One way to structure this book would be to embrace the reality of separation. It would be possible to devote individual chapters to 'early comedies', 'problem comedies', and 'romances' or to issues such as 'gender', 'race', and 'class'. *A Very Short Introduction* could have a section on 'world Shakespeare' describing the international reception of the comedies, or have sections on specific media, such as 'the comedies on film' or 'the comedies on the internet'. A more traditional approach might systematically tackle 'the sources of Shakespeare's comedies', 'the institution of the early modern playhouse', and 'the comedies as they first appeared in print'. All of these are useful categories and, one way or another, information about these topics has to make its way into this book.

Yet, however much the comedies differ, the approach I have taken is an attempt to define shared qualities rather than subdivisions.

With this objective in mind, my first chapter looks at the 'world' of Shakespearean comedy, isolating the distinctive way that its stories play out in space. Under the heading of 'wit', Chapter 2 considers Shakespeare's jokes, including puns, double meanings, and the psychology of laughter. The third chapter is about 'love', which—I argue—is not only a consistent concern in Shakespeare's comedy but also, more surprisingly, an original one. Chapter 4 is about 'time' and the strange ways in which Shakespeare manipulates it, from the neat one-day chronology of *The Comedy of Errors* (1594) to the sixteen years that are casually skipped over between the third and the fourth act of *The Winter's Tale* (1609–10). Finally, the fifth and longest chapter is about 'character', starting with E. M. Forster's memorable distinction in *Aspects of the Novel* between characters that are 'flat' and characters that are 'round'. More than anything else, I suggest, it is the way Shakespeare treats character that differs from his contemporaries and also from later writers of comedy; this is not to say, however, that his characters are straightforwardly more 'real'. As a conclusion to this book, I consider 'endings', covering not only the concluding scenes of Shakespeare's dramas but also the difficult question of the playwright's apparent abandonment of comic writing in the final years of his life. Overall, I will argue that Shakespeare had a more consistent idea of what comedy was than is now often asserted. Comedy was his mainstay, spreading not just across the eighteen or so plays that can be listed under that heading but, beyond this, into his non-dramatic poetry, his histories, and—most powerfully of all—into the tragedies.

Chapter 1
World

Into the forest

In point of fact, only two of Shakespeare's comedies—*A Midsummer Night's Dream* (1595) and *As You Like It* (1600)—are set predominantly in forests, yet the idea that his plays take place in nature and are somehow natural creations remains a dominant one (Figure 4). From the Restoration until well into the 20th century, critics were fond of contrasting the 'natural' Shakespeare with his apparently more learned and city-based contemporary Ben Jonson. Dryden in 1668 wrote that 'all the images of nature were still present' to Shakespeare and that 'he needed not the spectacles of books to read nature . . . he looked inwards, and found her there'. A hundred years later Dr Johnson still found such naturalness in the playwright, particularly in the comedies. They were, he said, 'natural and therefore durable', it was 'the uniform simplicity of primitive qualities' that gave them strength.

Scholars today are rightly suspicious of such characterizations of Shakespeare, who was the product of a classical and urban education, and who largely addressed a metropolitan audience. He was not a child of nature and his plays are not especially wooded (even *As You Like It*'s Arden has a thriving wool trade, so is far from being an absolute wilderness). Still, the popular intuition that the comedies are set in forests does have an element

4. John Macpherson, 'The Forest of Arden', in Frederick Gard Fleay, ed., *The Land of Shakespeare* (London: Bumpus, 1889), Folger Shakespeare Library.

of truth to it because, even when the action takes place in cities, they have a very forest-like sense of space.

Here the contrast with Jonson becomes instructive. Plays like *Volpone* (1606) or *The Alchemist* (1610), which shared a space with Shakespeare's comedies at the Globe playhouse, are not simply urban but architectural. Their action largely centres on a single room. Jonson's plots put immense pressure on a single location: as the play progresses more and more characters demand access, often under the dictates of a ticking clock. All the characters have a concrete sense of the street plan of the fiction; there are frequent references to place. Even Jonson's gulls have a degree of urban canniness, being wary of imposters and usually on the lookout for a quick buck. Disguise is thus potentially fallible (Volpone dressed up as a Mountebank in Venice, for example, worries 'is not the colour o' my beard and eyebrows / To make me known?'). This is all very different in Shakespeare, where nobody asks such questions, even when the dramatist chooses Venice as his locale.

The forest-like quality of Shakespeare's cities is not immediately obvious to readers, especially those who consult 19th- and 20th-century editions, because editors have a long tradition of adding locations to help readers to identify the physical placement of the action. It is thus, for example, that what is still the most recent Arden edition sets the scene for the start of *The Comedy of Errors* (1594):

> SCENE: *The play is set in Ephesus. The scene throughout represents an unlocalized street or 'mart' in front of three 'houses', structures or doors marked with the signs of the Courtesan's house (a Porcupine), the house of Antipholus of Ephesus (the Phoenix), and Priory (a cross or some religious emblem).*

This all sounds very authoritative. *The Comedy of Errors* is Shakespeare's most place-specific drama and the whole point of its plot is that two pairs of twins spend a single day in the same city, causing chaos through mistaken identity as they rush from person to person giving conflicting commands. Yet the 'scene' that the Arden editor gives us is a fantasy. The original printed text of the play gives no stage directions about location and early modern production would have varied enormously depending on the performance space used.

Even *The Comedy of Errors*, the most classical of the comedies, often floats free of its rigid exterior urban backdrop. Indeed at times Shakespeare creates a rather 'domestic' atmosphere on the stage. Act 3 Scene 2, for example, though it is not really set in any concrete location, feels like it is taking place inside the house of Antipholus of Ephesus (the twin who has just been locked out by his wife in the previous scene). Unbeknownst to the house owner, his identical brother is being entertained by his wife and servants, who mistake him for the master. The audience gets a sense of the interior of this house through references to the 'kitchen wench' and the presence of the wife and sister, even while the exits and entries of other characters still convey the fluidity of the street.

The scene cannot logically be tied to a single physical setting, it simply plays out on 'the stage'. Unsurprisingly, the stranger Antipholus of Syracuse feels he has come to a kind magical ocean—calling Luciana 'sweet mermaid' and 'siren', and waxing lyrical on this strange realm:

> Against my soul's pure truth why labour you
> To make it wander in an unknown field?
> Are you a god? Would you create me new?
> Transform me, then, and to your power I'll yield. (3.2.37–40)

As the action progresses, the city of Ephesus feels more and more like a forest: 'this the fairy land. O spite of spites, / We talk with goblins, elves and sprites' complains the servant Dromio of Syracuse (2.2.192–3). The 'Priory' (which the Arden editor identifies as one of the three 'houses' present at the play's opening) only comes into being in the final act as a kind of magical refuge. Logically, this Christian location (with an abbess who turns out to be the lost mother of the Antipholus twins) has no place in this ancient Greek city-state.

What is true of Ephesus in *The Comedy of Errors* (1594) is still truer of a place like Illyria in *Twelfth Night* (1601). This play oscillates between two courts or households: that of Orsino, Duke of Illyria, and that of Olivia, 'the daughter of a count' (1.2.31). The nature of these two places and the space between them is far from obvious. Is the Duke sovereign over Olivia's household? Does Olivia live in a palace or simply a grand house? What kind of distance separates these two centres of action and is it urban or is it wild? Any literal answer to these questions will end up feeling flatfooted. In *Twelfth Night* there is frequent mention of places: Olivia's garden with its 'box-tree' from which Sir Toby and his companions spy upon Malvolio; the 'streets' on which Sebastian is accused of brawling; the 'south suburbs' where Antonio lodges at an Inn, the Elephant; the 'dark room' in which Malvolio is tied up. This all feels urban and demarcated, but in practice the spaces are not so narrowly defined. The jester Feste, for example, moves easily from one location to another, taking part in the high jinx in Olivia's household but also being 'about the house' in Orsino's court (2.4.12). The long final scene of the play is likewise notoriously difficult to stage because it takes place in a kind of no-space: officers bring the arrested Antonio onto the stage as if they were in a law court; Olivia orders her servants about as if she is at home and mistress of the household; and when Sir Andrew Aguecheek and Sir Toby Belch burst in with cut heads demanding the services of a drunk surgeon named Dick it feels like we are suddenly in an English town. The stage is an Italianate court, a country house, and a rowdy street at the same moment, and when Feste concludes the play with his song 'hey, ho, the wind and the rain' we seem more in a forest than anywhere else (5.1.386).

Thanks to this fluid interchange of locations there is a good deal of overlap between Shakespeare's urban comedies and those that are genuinely set in a wilderness. *A Midsummer Night's Dream* (1595) is in this respect simply the ultimate instance of the conjunction of worlds that Shakespeare creates throughout his fictions, combining aristocrats with commoners, the magic with the prosaic, and the ancient with the contemporary. It is difficult to remember that this play is supposedly set in classical Greece in a wood outside Athens because Nick Bottom and the other rude mechanicals are so manifestly the product of a very different place and time. The special rules of the forest allow Shakespeare to create some bizarre scenarios, such as that of some 16th-century Englishmen performing a classical tragedy ('The most lamentable comedy, and most cruel death of Pyramus and Thisbe') in front of Theseus and Hypolita, who are actual characters from Greek Myth.

It is not simply that the timeless forest allows such meetings from across history, it also creates special rules of movement by which people meet only when the dramatist wants them to. Thus, in *A Midsummer Night's Dream*, characters repeatedly fall asleep at the instant before another enters. Titania, moreover, falls asleep

in the precise spot where the rude mechanicals have chosen
to rehearse. The forest seems infinitely large and at the same
time infinitely congested; it is the perfect blank slate stage.
Movement on the streets of Ephesus or Illyria is also like this:
twins meet only at the conclusion, at which point no walls can
keep them apart.

This strange quality of space is one of the reasons that there have
been so few critically acclaimed films made of the comedies.
Cinema is almost always a realist medium: as Michael Hattaway
puts it, its screen functions 'as a window on to a "real" world'.
This sense of solidity can work well for Shakespearean tragedy,
where oppressive locations such as Elsinore or Dunsinane can
supplement the interiority of characters like Hamlet or Macbeth.
Shakespeare's comedy, however, is often impoverished by choosing
a concrete location. Even Franco Zeffirelli's celebrated film of
The Taming of the Shrew, starring Richard Burton and Elizabeth
Taylor, loses a lot by fixing its action in an Italian town rather
than the play-within-a-play performance of the original text.
Amongst the most inventive solutions to this problem is that
offered by Adrian Noble's film of *A Midsummer Night's Dream*.
The action here is set in a magical house, played out in miniature
under tables or seen through a stovetop from the perspective of
a perplexed young boy. Noble's film kept close to the original 1994
RSC production that lay behind it, with frequent images of stage
sets, including a child's puppet theatre and a Victorian-style
playhouse for the performance by the rude mechanicals at the
close. Brilliantly, Noble's film creates the forest not through trees
but through a set of doors that rise out of and drop into the stage
floor, sometimes opening to reveal characters, sometimes just
empty space (see Figure 5). The doors evoke the tradition of
theatrical farce, but what we see is farce that defies the normal
rules of the genre. The play's lovers, Helena, Hermia, Demetrius,
and Lysander, repeatedly enter one free-floating door only to
emerge out of another that is entirely unconnected to it. This
surrealist quality of theatrical space perfectly encapsulates the

**5. 'Titania's Bower' from Adrian Noble's 1994 production of
A Midsummer Night's Dream, Shakespeare Birthplace Trust.**

nature of the Shakespearean forest: at once wild and domestic,
restricted and infinite. There is something dreamlike about all
Shakespeare's comedies—whether they are set in forests, courts, or
cities—and more than anything else this is a consequence of their
locational elasticity, bending properties of space and time.

Out of the court

Halfway through *As You Like It* (1600), the jester Touchstone,
who has travelled with Rosalind and Celia into the Forest of
Arden, strikes up a conversation with one of the natives, a
shepherd named Corin. 'How like you this shepherd's life?' asks
Corin, to which Touchstone gives this very equivocal reply:

> Truly, shepherd, in respect of itself, it is a good life; but in respect
> that it is a shepherd's life, it is naught. In respect that it is solitary,

I like it very well; but in respect that it is private, it is a very vile life.
Now in respect it is in the fields, it pleaseth me well; but in respect
it is not in the court, it is tedious. (3.2.13–18)

Touchstone's reply contains the paradoxical quality we find in the
world of Shakespearean comedy: it is of the court but also outside
it, there is regret for an exile from courtliness, but this exile is also
what allows comedy to thrive. The ensuing debate between Corin
and Touchstone continues to be marked by this odd conjunction.
Touchstone insists, for example, that Corin's manners, because
they are not the 'good manners' of the court must be 'wicked'
and that the shepherd's soul is thus 'in a parlous state' (3.2.40–3).
The debate between the two proceeds in an absurdly structured,
academic manner, with the participants asking formal questions:
'Your reason?', 'Instance, briefly', 'Come, instance', 'Shallow,
shallow', 'a better instance, I say. Come' (3.2.38, 50, 55–6). Thus,
even though Touchstone complains of being amongst rustics, we
as audience find ourselves in an intellectual space that is at least
halfway to court.

The conversation between Corin and Touchstone is a good example
of what William Empson called the 'trick of the old pastoral' of
'putting the complex into the simple'. At its most basic this involves
the 'gentle irony' of making outwardly naive characters express
elevated and educated thoughts. What Empson called 'the old
pastoral' was essentially an urban genre. Though it depicted
shepherds and other rustic folks and praised the simplicity of
nature, pastoral's conventions were highly stylized. Thus, in works
such as Edmund Spenser's *The Shepherd's Calender*, which
Shakespeare knew intimately, we find swains like Corin discussing
weighty topics (including art, love, theology, and politics) in
crafted poetic metres as they tend to their sheep. Bringing courtly
characters into this landscape was likewise conventional: it
prompted questions about the corruptness of civilization, about
the way inner nobility might express itself in nature, and about the
difference between men and beasts. Sir Philip Sidney's *Arcadia*,

which Shakespeare used several times as a source text, is grounded on that displacement. Its princes and princesses, by temporarily becoming foresters, learn new truths about themselves.

Shakespeare's forests are like courts and his cities are like forests; this strange inversion tells us much about the rules that govern his art. The formal disputation between Touchstone and Corin is typical of the exchanges that the dramatist embeds within natural settings: it is comparable, for example, to the debate about the relative merits of art and nature that is held between the disguised aristocrats Perdita and Polixenes in *The Winter's Tale* (4.4.79–108). A key component of Shakespeare's comic world, then, is pastoral, whether directly through sources such as Robert Greene's *Pandosto* (1588) or in a more diffuse manner through the importation of customs such as formal dialogue, gender disguise, and song. Plenty of other Renaissance dramatists made use of this strange neverland, twinning rusticity with academia, the most obvious example being John Lyly, whose plays—such as *Galatea* (1594) and *Love's Metamorphosis* (1590)—where a shaping influence on Shakespeare's work.

The combination of the courtly and the rural that is licensed through pastoral drama helps to resolve the contradictory responses found in early criticism of Shakespeare's comedies, which declared them wild and unlearned yet also somehow naturally cultured (much gentler than the hard world of Jonson's satires). George Meredith, in one of the wisest overall studies of comedy that has been written, began with a very conventional generalization when he wrote as follows:

> Shakespeare is a well-spring of characters which are saturated with the comic spirit; with more of what we will call blood-life than is to be found anywhere out of Shakespeare; and they are of this world, but they are of the world enlarged to our embrace by imagination, and by great poetic imagination. They are, as it were—I put it to suit my present comparison—creatures of woods and wilds, not in

walled towns, not grouped and toned to pursue a comic exhibition
of the narrower world of society.

There is something very appealing about this generalization, but
it does sit at odds Meredith's larger thesis about the nature of
comedy, which he sees as a profoundly cultivated genre. Because
Meredith argues that 'semi-barbarism' is anathema to comedy he
in fact has little specific to say about Shakespeare, whom he tends
to view as a self-schooled genius and great exception to the
standard rules.

In fact, Meredith's rules about the environment that allows comedy
to flourish are applicable to Shakespeare even if they look out of
place in the world of the forest. Not only does he require 'a society
of cultivated men and women', he also says that 'some degree of
social equality of the sexes' is necessary for comedy to thrive.
Meredith is thinking principally of parlour witticism: Jane Austen's
Emma and Mr Elton 'might walk straight into a comedy, were the
plot arranged for them', he observes. Austen's leisured, polite,
Regency splendour feels a very long way from the Globe playhouse
in Shakespeare's London, yet—strangely—the rules of pastoral did
create a forest version of the parlour on the Elizabethan stage. In
the fictive worlds of Arden or Illyria women disguised as boys
momentarily achieve the 'degree of social equality' that Meredith
specifies and thus become worthy participants in games of learned
folly such as the 'intellectual pleading of a doubtful cause'. Rosalind
(disguised as Ganymede) swapping witticisms with Orlando in
As You Like It is not so very different from Emma bantering with
Mr Elton in the drawing rooms of Jane Austen's novel.

If Shakespeare's comic creations are, as Meredith claims, not the
creatures of 'walled towns', they are not quite the creatures of
'woods and wilds' either. They have moved from the urban and
courtly to the natural, but they are always ready to move back. The
radical transitions that occur on the borders of Shakespeare's
green spaces make this point clearly. Those who enter can be

changed in an instant. The evil Duke Frederic in *As You Like It* (1600) is an extreme example. At the end of the play he is reported as arriving with a vast army, determined to find his brother and 'put him to the sword' (5.4.150). The magic of the forest, however, has its immediate effect. In the words of Jaques de Bois (a convenient second brother to Orlando who makes a functional appearance at this point in the play) he needed barely to set foot in the greenworld for all the rules of the court to disappear:

> to the skirts of this wild wood he came,
> Where, meeting with an old religious man,
> After some question with him was converted
> Both from his enterprise and from the world,
> His crown bequeathing to his banished brother,
> And all their lands restored to them again
> That were with him exiled. This to be true
> I do engage my life. (5.4.157–64)

The functionality of this change is so shameless that its absurdity is barely registered by the audience in a good production: we accept it simply as the dramatist's tying up of loose ends before the exiled Duke's party returns in triumph to the court. The pragmatic world of the walled town, however, can make a return in a less festive manner. *Love's Labour's Lost* (1594–5), too, sets its comedy in a kind of pastoral neverland, with the Queen of France obliged to lodge 'in the field' outside the gates of Navarre. Yet this play ends in no happy return to civility: the news of the Queen's father sends her for a year to 'a mourning house' and the loquacious Berowne to a 'hospital' to tend to the sick. Physical specificity marks the end of comedy in each case.

Shakespeare can make his cities, towns, and courts obey the spatial rules of the forest when he wants to (Windsor, in *The Merry Wives of Windsor*, for example, never really feels restricted and turns easily to a forest location at its close). At times, however, walls and doors do become a more material presence and comedy flows much less easily as a result. This is the case in the walled Troy of *Troilus and Cressida* (1602) or the dungeons of Vienna in *Measure for Measure* (1603). The council chambers, raised galleries, closets, and prisons of these locations infect the spirits of the protagonists—we are in a world of corrupt rulers, lowlife villains, and sexual disease. The conventional elements of comedy (disguise, substitution, marriage, the mockery of jesters) come to feel forced and artificial in these locations: Shakespeare makes difficult the things that seem effortless in the natural world. Thus, at the end of *Measure for Measure*, the deceitful Angelo converts to goodness with the same declared ease as Duke Frederick in *As You Like It*, but—lacking the magic of pastoral—he leaves no one convinced.

First place and second place

Many Shakespearean comedies start in a court and move out to the country: they end in this wild space outside the bounds of civilization, but with the promise of a festive return. Some, however, employ a more dynamic structure, where two distinct places are put in contrapuntal dialogue. *The Merchant of Venice* (1596–7) is a good example. The Venice and Belmont of this play are not only physically distant, the two locations effectively employ different sets of generic rules. The casket test that determines Portia's choice of husband is thus almost impossible to imagine in Venice. Belmont is a place where fairy-tale characters like Portia's other suitors—the Princes of Morocco and Aragon—are quite happy to sign up for absurd love trials in which failure to secure the right casket commits the chooser to an unmarried life. Such arrangements seem unlikely to pass the legal scrutiny of Venice's law courts: that city is a place of precisely worded contracts, not one of adventure and symbolism.

The generic rules of Sicilia and Bohemia in *The Winter's Tale* (1609–10) are likewise very different, not simply at the level of character behaviour but also as regards the tools that the dramatist employs in setting the scene. In Sicilia (the location of almost all of acts one to three) there are no songs or comic interludes and no absurd interventions from the world of nature (such as Bohemia's notorious 'exit pursued by a bear'). Sicilia is stark and formal: there are trials and diplomatic conversations and in the final stages of the play it is a place of mystical faith. Bohemia is much earthier: it is a land of pastoral comedy whose characters and landscape are by turns classical and homespun. The following scruffy verse from the classically named but English-feeling Autolycus gives an impression of its mood:

> The lark, that tirra-lirra chants,
>> With heigh, with heigh, the thrush and the jay,
> Are summer songs for me and my aunts
>> While we lie tumbling in the hay. (4.3.9–12)

The 'aunts' here are girlfriends or mistresses. This word, along with the singer's references to hay-tumbling and English bird names, lends a distinctly non-Mediterranean cadence to the song. In line with this theme of merry England, the sexual codes of Bohemia are decidedly more relaxed than those of Sicilia, where even Hermione's chaste entreaties raise suspicions in the King. The to-and-fro between Bohemia and Sicilia thus gains thematic significance. Through his contrasting worlds, Shakespeare pitches sterility against the fertile, tragedy against comedy, winter against spring.

The tendency to set a first world against a second word is distinctive to Shakespeare. His contemporaries tended to be more absolute in their sense of setting, even if those settings were, just like Shakespeare's, gloriously anachronistic (with fashionable Italian braggarts roaming every location from 6th-century Arabia to ancient Britain). Shakespeare's willingness to set one world alongside another takes him to the margins of comedy and into the territory of other modes. Thus, if *The Winter's Tale* is predominantly a romance rather than a comedy, we could say that its comedy is restricted to the land of Bohemia, whose borders are quite strongly policed. Something similar might be said of the *Henry IV* plays, which also operate according to a pattern of contrasting worlds. Falstaff is Shakespeare's greatest comic creation and can function in all environments, but it's in the London backstreets and in rural Gloucestershire that he is truly at home. In these places—as in Arden—a temporary relaxation of social distinctions seems possible: disguise and role-play are licensed and there is a reprieve from the logic of time.

Henry IV, Part 1 thus begins with a scene of high politics in which news from the kingdom's borders and urgent demands for action come to the fore. In contrast to this, scene two, located loosely in the London underworld, opens appropriately on Falstaff's line 'Now, Hal, what time of day is it, lad?' and the Prince's repost, which insists on the absence of time in the knight's worldview:

> What a devil has thou to do with the time of the day? Unless hours were cups of sack, and minutes capons, and clocks the tongues of bawds, and dials the signs of leaping-houses, and the blessed sun himself a fair hot wench in flame-coloured taffeta, I see no reason why thou shouldst be so superfluous to demand the time of the day. (1.2.6–12)

Hal's speech here anticipates Orlando's declaration in *As You Like It* that there is 'no clock in the forest', just as Falstaff's rejoinder, 'Let us be "Diana's foresters", "gentlemen of the shade", "minions of the moon"' (1.2.25–6), confirms the Arden-like qualities of the world he opens up for the young prince. The whole Gadshill robbery escapade that follows is in line with that shift in the ground rules. It takes place in a suitably rural setting outside the city and involves Hal and his companion Poins robbing Falstaff in disguise. The knight's later account of the incident—full of ludicrous exaggeration and special pleading—confirms George Meredith's dictum that the germ of comedy is to be found in the intellectual pleading of a doubtful cause.

The twinned worlds of the *Henry IV* plays confirm the peculiar spatial qualities of Shakespeare's comic drama. In this kind of space no meeting is inevitable, time is expandable, and a law of nature seems invariably to supply physical need. Falstaff's clock counts only sack and capons (i.e. wine and fattened roosters) just as Sir Toby Belch in *Twelfth Night* (1601) eats and drinks at all hours and insists that 'to go to bed after midnight is to go to bed betimes' (2.3.8–9). The fat knights have much in common, above all their opposition to a sense of measuredness and calculation. In this respect Malvolio the Puritan represents the same target as the Machiavellian politicians of the *Henry IV* plays. The difference, however, is that Sir Toby inhabits the true comic space of Illyria, where no army can penetrate, whereas the Falstaff of the Henriad must ultimately bend to historical rules of space and time.

Chapter 2
Wit

Quibbles

'A quibble is to Shakespeare what luminous vapours are to the traveller; he follows it at all adventures, it is sure to lead him out of his way, and sure to engulf him'. Thus wrote Dr Johnson in 1765. At least since William Hazlitt's devastating critique of Johnson's opinions on Shakespeare in 1817, we have not taken such criticism very seriously. Still, reading Shakespeare's comedies back-to-back in a few sittings, even the most ardent Shakespearean begins to feel that Johnson had a point. 'A quibble' is a pun or a play on words and Shakespeare is full of them. Many are rather alien to modern sensibilities. They tend to be sexist and obsessed with cuckoldry, with the same jokes appearing again and again. In annotated editions they generate long explanatory footnotes; in production they are often cut. While Shakespeare's comic worlds seem eternal and endlessly adaptable, his quibbles are more time-bound, not only in their meanings but in the attitudes they convey. We may no longer agree with Johnson that 'a quibble was to him the fatal Cleopatra for which he lost the world, and was content to lose it', but Shakespeare's wordplay does present a challenge. Is it really compatible with the vision of a writer whose poetry always 'shone with the beams of native genius' that Hazlitt and other Romantic critics present?

So where do we find Shakespeare's quibbles and do they really—as Johnson contends—distract the playwright from his real business because their fascination is 'irresistible', leaving 'his work unfinished' as wordplay takes over from plot? The case for the prosecution will find some damning evidence in *The Two Gentlemen of Verona*, which is possibly Shakespeare's first play. Like many of the early comedies, it is filled with set piece exchanges between servants that are an accommodating vehicle for verbal jests:

> SPEED: How now, Signor Lance? What news with our mastership?
> LANCE: With my master's ship? Why, it is at sea.
> SPEED: Well, your old vice still, mistake the word. What news then in your paper?
> LANCE: The blackest news that ever thou heard'st.
> SPEED: Why, man? How 'black'?
> LANCE: Why, as black as ink. (3.1.276–83)

This is hardly the brilliance we expect of Shakespeare, still less 'the union of the poet and the philosopher' and the 'organic regularity' in which 'there is a law which all the parts obey, conforming themselves to the outward symbols and manifestations of the essential principle' that the great romantic poet-critic Samuel Taylor Coleridge commends. Lance's 'old vice' of 'mistake the word', which runs on for many pages, is likely to try the patience of even the most committed Shakespeare fan.

Early audiences were apparently much more receptive to this kind of wordplay. Immediately after Shakespeare's death those looking back on the past generation of comic writers made an increasingly clear distinction between 'humour' and 'wit' as qualities exciting laughter and the playwright was very much celebrated for his wit. Humour, as William Congreve explained, was essentially about character and the best examples of humoural comedy came from Ben Jonson. The character of

Morose from Jonson's *Epicoene* (1610) is a perfect example of a humour: a man totally obsessed by his own health (above all his hatred of loud noises) and thus a suitable object of satire. Wit, on the other hand, was much more about cleverness, including cleverness with language: things 'surprisingly and pleasantly' spoken as Congreve puts it. This pleasant aspect of wit is almost the opposite of satire and may be found in any kind of character: according to Congreve, 'from a witty man they are expected and even a fool may be permitted to stumble on 'em by chance'. Shakespeare, although Congreve does not explicitly say so, is much more a 'wit' author than a creator of 'humour' in the 17th-century sense. John Dryden made this contrast between Jonson and Shakespeare a key pivot in his account of the preceding generation of comic dramatists. For the former 'humour was his proper sphere, and in that he delighted most to represent mechanic people [...] if I would compare him with Shakespeare, I must acknowledge him the more correct poet, but Shakespeare the greater wit'.

When Dryden says that Shakespeare is 'many times flat, insipid, his comic wit degenerating into clenches' he is probably thinking of cases such as the quoted exchange between Speed and Lance in *The Two Gentleman of Verona*. Overall, however, he finds Shakespeare's wittiness an abundant natural faculty: 'the advantage of Shakespeare's wit' was a great transforming inheritance for 17th-century English playwrights: it allowed them to escape the harshness of traditional comedy and replace it with delight. The light, purposeless quality of Shakespeare's wit (in contrast to the instructive model championed by Jonson) was greatly loved by 17th-century audiences. It is for this reason, for example, that William Davenant lifted the Beatrice and Benedick plot (with its 'merry war' of wit between two sparring lovers) from *Much Ado About Nothing* and pasted it into the plot of *Measure for Measure* to produce the successful new play *The Law Against Lovers* in 1662. When we look at Beatrice's wit we find something subtler than the Lance-Speed banter, but it is still fundamentally a game of 'mistake the word'.

Although it is light hearted, wit of this kind is perceived as a threat by the play's other characters. As her cousin Hero puts it, Beatrice 'turns every man the wrong side out':

> If I should speak,
> She would mock me into air, O, she would laugh me
> Out of myself, press me to death with wit. (3.1.68, 74–6)

The 'turning' or reversal that Beatrice achieves operates at the level of both language and character. Thus, when Benedick is commended as 'a good soldier too, lady', she twists the messenger's intention: 'a good soldier to a lady, but what is he to a lord?' (1.1.51–3). Wit of this kind is almost a poetic faculty and indeed the word 'wit' was often used as a word to describe creative genius in Shakespeare's age. The grander cases of Beatrice's comic invention confirm that literary aspect, they are made up of 'conceits' in the same way that Metaphysical poetry (such as that by John Donne) is built on conceits. The Penguin *Dictionary of Literary Terms* describes the Renaissance conceit as follows: 'a fairly elaborate figurative device of a fanciful kind which often incorporates metaphor, simile, hyperbole or oxymoron and which is intended to surprise and delight by its wit and ingenuity'. Beatrice and Benedick, skilled architects of such devices, turn frequently to the resources of hyperbole and metaphor as they joust with words. This, for example, is how Beatrice first addresses Benedick in the play:

> BEATRICE: I wonder that you will still be talking, Signor. Nobody marks you.
> BENEDICK: What, my dear Lady Disdain! Are you yet living?
> BEATRICE: Is it possible Disdain should die, while she hath such meet food to feed it as Signor Benedick?
> Courtesy itself must convert to Disdain if you come in her presence. (1.1.110–16)

To give Beatrice the allegorical title Lady Disdain is already a leap of the imagination, but what is clever about her reply is that it takes this personification and runs with it: not only is the deity alive, she is kept in rude health by Benedick's presence, which has the alchemical power to turn even Courtesy to Disdain. Turning the earthy Benedick, a 'valiant trencher-man' who 'hath an excellent stomach', into food for an abstract deity has a brilliant absurdity to it. We are in a world a little like that of Donne's satires, where the skill of constructing an insult is taken to an abstruse intellectual level even while it remains physically crude. It is in this spirit that Donne writes of a poet who imitates his verses 'For if one eat my meat, though it be known / the meat was mine, th' excrement is his own' and of a lady who aspires to beauty 'Though all her parts be not in th' usual place, / She hath yet an anagram of a good face'. This is very much the kind of turning-inside-out at which Beatrice excels.

In one sense, then, Shakespeare's wit is—as Congreve professes—intellectually and morally purposeless; it is simply an entertaining game that clever people enjoy. But wit can, nevertheless, also form part of the 'organic regularity' of Shakespeare's creations that Coleridge so much admired. Even in *The Two Gentlemen of Verona* there is a thematic purpose to the relentless jests and reversals that make up the play's language and plot. As we can tell from the names of the lead male characters, Valentine and Proteus, this is a play about love and transformation and the twisting of language that marks the speech of all its characters is perfectly congruent with that theme.

The second scene of *The Two Gentlemen of Verona*, featuring Julia and her maid Lucetta, is a good example. The wit here has a musical regularity, as the women exchange paired lines, half lines, and full lines, and run through the scale of double meanings on a whole series of musical terms: 'note', 'sharp', 'flat', 'base', 'burthen'. The scene ends with Julia tearing up the letter over which the women have been arguing and then attempting to fit it together again piece by piece. In itself the scene is an airy nothing but in context it is a perfect synecdoche for the plot, which likewise works like a set of counterpoint variations, with letters misdirected, misascribed, torn up, and falsified. All characters in *The Two Gentlemen of Verona* seem addicted to such twisting of words from their original meaning, thus giving coherence to the topic of constant change.

In more emotionally complex plays like *Much Ado About Nothing* the moments where wit seems inappropriate can also carry weight. Here the standard devices of comedy, such as the ingenuity of wily servants, mistaken identity, and a man wooing in another's name (all of which we see in *The Two Gentlemen of Verona*) end up being employed with evil intent. The place of wit in a comedy that is all about false accusations of infidelity, then, takes on a leaden aspect (indeed Shakespeare would test such wit to destruction in the tragedy of *Othello* five years on). Most grating of all in *Much Ado About Nothing* is the attempted jollity of Don Pedro and Claudio immediately after they have shamed the falsely accused Hero and left her for dead. The two men then seek out Benedick in search of entertainment in a manner that is unforgivably crass:

> CLAUDIO: We have been up and down to seek thee, for we are high-proof melancholy and would fain have it beaten away. Wilt thou use thy wit?
> BENEDICK: It is in my scabbard. Shall I draw it?
> DON PEDRO: Dost thou wear thy wit by thy side?
> CLAUDIO: Never any did so, though very many have been beside their wit. I will bid thee draw as we do the minstrels, draw to please us. (5.1.123–30)

Don Pedro and Claudio's wit here is, on Shakespeare's part, intentionally feeble: first, the former attempts a play on the phrase 'besides one's wit' (i.e. at the end of one's wits with frustration) then Claudio tries to cap this by suggesting that Benedick has lost his wits (i.e. has gone crazy in his love for Beatrice), but neither jest comes off. The 'turn' from melancholy to laughter is not achieved.

What the references to wit here do reveal, however, is the violence that lies in all comedy, the aggression that made Thomas Hobbes famously define laughter as 'sudden glory' over a defeated rival. To quote his assessment of wit a little more generously:

> Men laugh at jests, the wit wereof always consisteth in the elegant discovering and conveying to our minds some absurdity of another: and in this case also the passion of laughter proceedeth from the sudden imagination of our own odds and eminency: for what is else the recommending of our selves to our own good opinion, by comparison with another man's infirmity or absurdity? For when a jest is broken upon our selves, or friends of whose dishonour we participate, we never laugh thereat.

There is much to link Hobbes's statement here with the confrontation between Claudio and Benedick, which contains—even in its blunt humour—the atavistic origins of wit. On the one hand, Count Claudio's sallies, though friendly in spirit, denigrate a social inferior: comparing Benedick to minstrels who 'draw to please us' must sting, especially because it recalls Beatrice's earlier mockery of him as 'the Prince's jester' (2.1.127). On the other hand, the Count's vocabulary—'beaten away', 'draw', and later 'thou hast mettle enough in thee to kill care'—confess that Benedick's wit is the greater weapon. As Claudio and Don Pedro continue to prattle their wit becomes ever more feeble, particularly when the latter begins to tell a long anecdote about 'how Beatrice praised thy wit the other day'. In this context Benedick's stark determination to keep his wit in his scabbard on this occasion is an act of power. The quibbles that seem to distract Shakespeare, then, can be a shaping force not only in his plots but also in the emotional arc of his plays. This is not to say that he never overdoes it; few would feel any poorer for the loss of Speed and Lance.

Jokes and the unconscious

The linguist Victor Raskin is responsible for one of the most extended academic discussions of verbal humour and—after a hundred pages of overview, made up of systematic subsections complete with formulae—he concludes with the following 'general hypothesis':

> A text can be characterized as a single-joke-carrying text if both of the conditions in (108) are satisfied.
> (108) (i) The text is compatible, fully or in part, with two different scripts
> (ii) The two scripts with which the text is compatible are opposite in the special sense defined in Section 4.

There is inevitably something comic about a theory of jokes that takes itself quite this seriously; section 4 is very long and certainly defies summary in a *Very Short Introduction to Shakespeare's Comedies*. Luckily, however, Raskin tells a joke to illustrate his point:

> 'Is the doctor at home?' the patient asked in his bronchial whisper. 'No,' the doctor's young and pretty wife whispered in reply. 'Come right in.'

The joke is funnier than many by Shakespeare. It also helps to illustrate what Raskin means by 'scripts' in his general hypothesis and what he means by the 'special sense defined in Section 4'. By 'scripts' Raskin means something like 'social contexts' or 'specialised vocabularies'. The scripts implied in the joke that he gives as an example are (i) the conventional behaviour in a doctor's surgery; and (ii) the behaviour expected while pursuing a clandestine affair. These scripts are 'compatible' in that they are both situations where one is likely to whisper. They are also opposite in the 'special sense' of being simultaneously like and unlike each other because feeling bronchial in a doctor's surgery is the very opposite of feeling sexually excited, but the world of doctors and nurses is nevertheless imbued with innuendo and sexual possibility.

Raskin's explanation is a useful starting point for understanding Shakespeare's verbal comedy. Here, for example, is the dialogue in *Much Ado About Nothing* that occurs when the newly arrived Don Pedro first spots Hero at her father's side:

> DON PEDRO: I think this is your daughter.
> LEONATO: Her mother hath many times told me so.
> BENEDICK: Were you in doubt, sir, that you asked her?
> LEONATO: Signor Benedick, no, for then you were a child
> (1.1.98–102)

There are three social 'scripts' implied by this conversation: (i) the moment when one first sees a young woman alongside her father; (ii) the situation where a doting mother praises her daughter to her husband; and (iii) the situation where a man suspects his wife of sleeping with another man. These are three situations in which it is appropriate for someone to assert that a specific girl is her father's daughter. They are compatible in this sense, but in the 'special sense' of involving radically incompatible sorts of intimacy they are opposed.

The 'special sense' here is important and helped make the joke funny to an early modern public. I suspect, however, that it is much less funny for a 21st-century audience, at least in the West. Why this likely discrepancy? Here Freud's classic psychoanalytic study *Jokes and their Relation to the Unconscious* casts some light. Freud makes a distinction between 'the comic', 'humour', and 'jokes'. Physical things can be 'comic': the exaggerated movements of clowning being the obvious example. Benedick gasping and sighing in surprise as he hears (via the scripted conversation of Don Pedro, Claudio, and Leonato) that Beatrice is in love with him is comic in this sense. 'Humour', for Freud, is more about emotion and is centred on the self: 'pity, anger, pain, and so on', he says, can be made humorous if the sufferer does not take them seriously. Benedick is thus being humorous when, following his gulling by the comic conspirators, he tells the audience 'I will be horribly in love' (2.3.222–3). In practice there is overlap between all of Freud's categories, but he makes a telling observation when he states that jokes alone involve the unconscious: they depend on a 'double meaning' but also on 'inhibition', a secret connection and disconnection between things. 'The joke, it may be said, is the contribution made to the comic from the realm of the unconscious', states Freud.

Freud's analysis may help explain why Benedick's clowning and humorous self-mockery remain funny for a modern audience and why the endless jokes about cuckolds, perhaps, are not. It is always dangerous to generalize about the beliefs of a society, but it is fair to say that the male intellectual elite of the Renaissance tended to hold two potentially opposed convictions: first, that a woman's virtue was more or less identical to her having no sexual feelings; second, a misogynistic fear that all women were voracious and insatiable in their lust. We certainly find these two statements asserted again and again by characters in Shakespeare's plays (and indeed by the speakers in his poems). Female desire, then, is a taboo in early modern England and taboos perform an important function in jokes as they are understood by Freud.

Joke work, for Freud, is doing the same thing as 'dream work': it gives pleasure from a thing that is really not allowed. The economy of a joke creates a short of 'short-circuit', where, before we realize fully what a joke is implying the statement it makes is denied. To quote one last time from *Jokes and their Relation to the Unconscious*:

> The psychogenesis of jokes has taught us that the pleasure in a joke is derived from play with words or from the liberation of nonsense,

and that the meaning of the joke is merely intended to protect that pleasure from being done away with by criticism. (131)

For a joke to work it must contain novelty and cause momentary bewilderment and, importantly, the teller and hearer must share the same inhibitions. If we look at the world depicted in *Much Ado About Nothing* we find a simultaneous *fixation on* and *denial of* sex. The play's very title titillates with this double possibility; it assures an audience of the absence of real wrongdoing, but it also slyly gives them a moment of mental voyeurism through an allusion to 'vagina' (as Hamlet says in response of Ophelia's use of the word 'nothing': 'that's a fair thought to lie between a maid's legs').

Like the play's title, the joke about Leonato's being told that Hero is his daughter is a synecdoche (or 'part for a whole') for the action of the play. Again and again, the play's jokes play a game of hide and seek with female fidelity; so prevalent is it in the depiction of women that we might almost call it a fetish. In the 'open' part of the play, it is only a villain like Don John who could falsely accuse a bride of cheating her husband, but in the 'hidden' part of the play (in its 'joke work') that accusation is a constant refrain. Amazingly, the joke about the married man as a horned cuckold is still there in the penultimate speech made by Benedick: 'Prince, thou art sad, get thee a wife, get thee a wife. There is no staff more reverend than one tipped with horn' (5.4.121–3).

Robert Armin versus Will Kemp

Many aspects of Shakespeare's comedy remain constant; there are certainly cuckold jokes from the earliest plays to the last: look up the word 'horn' in a Shakespeare concordance and you will find well over forty feeble jests on the matter in the comedies alone. But there are also developments over the course of a career that ran for well over two decades: the earliest plays are more lyrical (more obviously filled with poetry); the middle ones (from around

1600 to 1605) contain harsher satire; and the late plays (written after 1607) have a fairy-tale aspect and are generally referred to as 'romances' and not as comedies at all. The factors shaping these changes are various: the influence of rival playwrights; physical changes to the playhouse; and, no doubt, even the unknowable evolution of the dramatist's mood and personal convictions over time. One very striking change, though, comes with a change of personnel at the turn of the century, because in 1600 Shakespeare's longstanding lead comic actor, Will Kemp, was replaced by a very different performer: the diminutive and satirical writer-performer Robert Armin. This shift produced an immediate alteration in the way that Shakespeare used wit.

Much Ado About Nothing was printed in 1600, roughly two years after it first appeared on the stage. This was a Quarto publication, much like a modern paperback, as opposed to the larger Folio of the complete dramatic works that was printed by the actors as a tribute to Shakespeare after his death. The Quarto was set from the author's working manuscript, sometimes called 'foul papers', and it still contains the names of a set of actors to whom Shakespeare assigned the parts as he wrote. Especially noteworthy is Will Kemp's role as Dogberry: the clumsy, misspeaking police constable who pursues the malefactors (or 'auspicious persons' as he calls them) responsible for Hero's unwarranted disgrace. Misspeaking and malapropism had long been a staple of the parts that Shakespeare wrote for this actor. Dogberry talks of the villains being 'condemned into everlasting redemption' (4.2.53–4) just as an earlier Kemp character, Bottom in *A Midsummer Night's Dream* (1595), commends 'the flowers of odious savours sweet' (3.1.76). A huge physical presence, brilliant at self-mockery and clowning, Kemp (see Figure 1) was the perfect actor to embody such bumbling, goodhearted chumps.

Armin (see Figure 6) was radically different as a performer, and from *As You Like It* (1600) onwards he allowed Shakespeare to create a series of superior tricksters, often dressed in motley,

THE
History of the two Maids of More-clacke,

VVith the life and simple maner of IOHN
in the Hospitall.

Played by the Children of the Kings
Maiesties Reuels.

VVritten by ROBERT ARMIN, seruant to the Kings
most excellent Maiestie.

LONDON,
Printed by *N.O.* for *Thomas Archer*, and is to be sold at his
shop in Popes-head Pallace. 1 6 0 9.

**6. Robert Armin, from the frontispiece of Armin's play *The Two Maids
of Moreclack* (1609), Huntington Library.**

termed 'fools' rather than 'clowns'. Where Kemp had been happy to have audiences laugh *at* him as much as *with* him, Armin was a more self-conscious comic, often claiming a moral purpose to his jests. The actor's first part for the company, Touchstone, is already a showcase for this new more acerbic drama. As Jaques says of this character: 'I must have liberty / Withal, as large a charter as the wind, / To blow on whom I please, for so fools have / [to] Cleanse the foul body of th'infected world' (2.7.47–9, 60). Whether either Touchstone or Armin takes this moral role seriously is an open question, but they certainly lay claim to it whenever they can.

Another distinguishing point of Armin's wit is that it is avowedly courtly, as opposed to the country wit of the clown. Touchstone is very much presented as a jester who has spent time in royal circles. It is this that allows him to offer court satire, for example in his extended set-piece routine on the seven 'degrees of the lie' (5.4.86–7). The contrast with the dramatist's earlier writing is set out with particular clarity in the rivalry between Touchstone and the country clown William, whose name is surely in part an in-joke on Shakespeare's earlier comic lead. Touchstone speaks of his wit from the first instant of spotting William:

> TOUCHSTONE: It is meat and drink to me to see a clown.
> By my troth, we that have good wits have much to
> answer for. We shall be flouting; we cannot hold. (5.1.10–12)

William's own notion of having 'a pretty wit' falls a long way short of Touchstone's and the jester's 'flouting' of his adversary is a specifically oratorical triumph. Quite the opposite of the stumbling Will Kemp, Armin/Touchstone mocks William through 'a figure in rhetoric' that shows off a command of Latin and a resplendent vocabulary:

> TOUCHSTONE: Therefore, you clown, abandon—which is in the vulgar,
> leave—the society—which in the boorish is company—

of this female—which in the common is woman; which
together is, abandon the society of this female, or,
clown, thou perishest. (5.1.46–50)

A clearer riposte to the tradition of Kemp can hardly be imagined
and nor can a clearer advertisement for a fresh, verbally intense,
form of wit.

Armin was himself a prolific writer, one who loved verbal
invention, absurdity, and also rather cruel forms of practical
joking aimed at humiliation. In this respect, William gets off
lightly from the wit contest, simply departing with a humble 'God
rest you merry, sir'. Subsequent Armin jesters, such as Thersites in
Troilus and Cressida (1602) or Lavatch in *All's Well That Ends
Well* (1604–5), are harder edged and thus more in the spirit of
Armin's pamphlets: they needle their interlocutors or rail at their
folly, leaving characters like the vain boaster Paroles fearfully
exposed. The most memorable victim of Armin's trickery, however,
is Malvolio, Lady Olivia's 'puritan' steward in *Twelfth Night* (1601).
Here too is a figure with a pompous sense of his own superiority
who is subsequently brought low.

Through a false trail of letters (not entirely unlike the scheme to
trick Beatrice and Benedick in *Much Ado About Nothing*) Malvolio
is brought to believe that the mistress of the house is in love with
him, a belief that causes him to behave in bizarre ways. Eventually,
he ends up locked in a dark room diagnosed as a victim of
madness and it is here that he is fully at the mercy of Feste, the
part that Armin originally took. As a licensed Fool ministering to
a supposed madman, Feste is able to heap paradoxes on his
victim. He asks questions such as 'are you not mad indeed, or do
you but counterfeit?', to which there is no rational answer. And
when Malvolio insists 'I am as well in my wits, fool, as thou art'
Feste can twist the situation by insisting 'But as well? Then you
are mad indeed, if you be no better in your wits than a fool'
(4.2.90–2). Perhaps still more intimidating for Malvolio is Feste's

production of nonsense, such as his denial of the prison's darkness
with the claim that 'it hath bay windows transparent as barricadoes'
and 'clerestories towards the south-north' that are 'as lustrous
as ebony' (4.2.37–9). Obviously, neither barricades nor ebony are
transparent, and there is no such direction as the south-north.
In the end, Malvolio's reaction to this humiliation comes close to a
genuine loss of selfhood; the assault of wit destroys him and he
ends up being described as a 'poor fool' by Olivia and vowing to be
'revenged on the whole pack of you' (5.1.374).

For Armin, wit was always twinned with folly or madness. His
most successful book, *Fool upon Fool* (1600), described the lives
of six 'fools', at least one of whom was still alive 'well known of
many'. He gathered anecdotes of their behaviour: the terrible
punishments they suffered, but also the victories that they
achieved over the ordinary world. Wit in the plays that came after
Armin's arrival in the company, therefore, is something a little
different from the wit in the first decade of Shakespeare's
compositions. It becomes wilder, less decorous, and more
dangerous for those at whom it is bent.

Shakespearean 'Wit', unlike 'World', is not easy to reconcile with
21st-century conventions: it can seem forced, obscure, and
artificial; it is linked to prejudices that are hopefully out-dated;
and it often involves cruelty of a kind that we rarely encounter in
contemporary popular comedy. The difficulty of Shakespeare's wit,
however, is also a hidden resource of his writing. Returning to its
original context can revive and transform drama that may
outwardly appear familiar and safe.

Chapter 3
Love

Getting the girl

The cruelty of wit can give a bitter edge to Shakespearean comedy, but that bitterness is generally balanced with a sweeter element: the narrative drive towards love. One simple way of dividing the comedies from other genres is to pick out those that end on marriage or the clear prospect of it: the list in the Folio and several other candidates for the title of 'comedy' all pass muster on this count. Sometimes marriage is a clear endpoint and uncomplicatedly joyous; those plays where marriage comes early or remains an ambiguous prospect—*All's Well That Ends Well*, *Love's Labour's Lost*, and *Measure for Measure*—are, unsurprisingly, much more downbeat in tone. This all seems pretty obvious. The pairing of love with marriage, however, is less self-evident as an ingredient for comedy than the old song suggests.

The classical New Comedy authored by Plautus and Terence that Shakespeare read at school was certainly very often centred on the pursuit of a girl. As I noted in my introduction, these plays built their ingenious plots from a set of stock characters: the young man (*adulescens*); the old man (*senex*); the eligible young woman (*virgo*); the courtesan (*meretrix*); and the wily servant (*servus callidus*) being the five most important out of a larger set. The standard template was that of an *adulescens* desiring a *virgo* or *meretrix*, with a *senex* blocking that prospect and of a *servus callidus* inventing a clever mechanism through which the young man ends up getting what he wants. Plautus's play *Mercator*, or *The Merchant*, is a suitably basic example. Charinus, the young son of a merchant, has fallen in lust with a slave girl, whom he has bought and brought home to Athens. Here Charinus's father, Demipho, sees the girl and asks after her. Charinus's slave then tries to save his master's blushes by saying that the girl is a gift from the son to his mother, which Demipho takes as a licence to pursue her on his own account. Various bits of confusion, including rival bidding for the slave girl, follow, but Charinus and his slave-mistress are reunited in the end. In this case there is no *virgo* (Pasicompsa is sexually experienced and decidedly flirty), but even where such characters do exist in the story they very rarely appear on the stage.

European audiences in the Renaissance required plots that had a greater role for women. Plays like *Mercator* were widely known and performed in academic contexts, but slavery and the wider unsentimental attitude to sexuality of classical antiquity could not be transferred wholesale onto the vernacular stage. The various kinds of Italian *comedia* thus changed slaves into servants and used Christian marriage (or at least romantic love) as a context for confusion and double dealing, while retaining much of the infrastructure of the *senex versus adulescens* rivalry. The multi-authored play *Gl' Ingannati* (*The Deceived*), set in Modena in the year of its first performance (1531), was a much-imitated example. Its central plot concerns a virtuous young woman, Leila, who falls in love with a young man called Flamminio. Standing in the way of their happy union there is an old man, Gherardo, whom Leila's father wishes her to marry, and also the small matter of Flamminio's passion for a rival, Isabella. These adverse circumstances force Leila to disguise herself as a pageboy and it is in this way that she eventually gains the marriage that she seeks.

Gl' Ingannati is clearly much closer to Shakespearean comedy than is *Mercato*: it is an obvious influence on *Twelfth Night* and probably also on the other girls-disguised-as-boys plots of *Two Gentlemen of Verona* and *As You Like It*. This summary of its plot, however, is a bit misleading, because the main theme of *Gl' Ingannati* is not really love. With the exception of Lelia and Flamminio (whose respective infatuation is absolute if stereotypical) the characters in this play are self-serving: Lelia's father wishes to dispose of his daughter; Gherardo is a white-bearded lecher; Isabella is lustful and unfaithful; and there are also various bawdy servant women and a *miles gloriosus* (braggart soldier) to throw into the mix. Even Flamminio expresses little passion for Lelia when he switches to her from Isabella and just moments before their marriage (while he still thinks her a pageboy) he pledges to take the 'boy' and 'cut off his lips and his ears and gouge out one of his eyes' so that he can send them to the woman he has lost. This is very much the hard, mercantile world of the Italian city, where the *virgo* is the prize of the best-qualified gallant.

There were plenty of English plays written in Shakespeare's lifetime that had the mood of *Gl' Ingannati*. William Haughton's *Englishmen for my Money*, performed at the Rose playhouse in 1598 is a good example, as is George's Chapman's *All Fools* of the same year. These plays have a love interest but they are not really about relationships, their main object is the triumph of wit over the blocking *sennex* or *pantaloon*. They anticipate the world of Restoration Comedy with its farcical action and intolerance of sentiment. True, Shakespeare's plays also feature impecunious young men who set out to marry for money and who get the better of older fathers who have cash: *The Taming of the Shrew* and *The Merchant of Venice* are good examples of this kind of plot. Those plays are, respectively, misogynist and anti-Semitic and they share the materialistic ethos of *Gl' Ingannati*, *Englishmen for my Money*, and *All Fools*. Many Shakespearean comedies, however, manage to give a very different impression, and even in *The Merchant of Venice* there is a relational quality that manages to make it more than a straightforward narrative of youth's victory over aged wealth.

Shakespearean comedy is about getting the girl or the boy, but it is also about love, and one ingredient that makes this possible is the sonnet. Hopeless examples are penned by a whole series of lovers: Berowne in *Love's Labour's Lost* (1594–5); Benedick in *Much Ado About Nothing* (1598); and Orlando in *As You Like It* (1600) to name but a few. These are not goal-oriented adventurers or experienced gallants, but foolish, infatuated dolts. Love strikes them like an arrow from Cupid (literally so in the case of the love potion that Puck applies to his victims in *A Midsummer Night's Dream*). There are examples of that kind of sudden total love madness in the plays of John Lyly, who wrote a few years before Shakespeare and influenced him a great deal. Yet to the classical metamorphic power of love in Lyly Shakespeare adds something extra: the medieval tradition of the knight and his lady, the tradition of courtly love, which is also there as an influence on the sonnet. Orlando's obsession with Rosalind in *As You Like It* has that origin, one source being *Orlando Furioso*, an Italian epic romance poem with a lovesick hero at its centre.

Such a rich blend of influences goes to produce something novel: a form that we might today call Romantic Comedy. A key part of this form is the depiction of infatuation that is somewhat misplaced in its object, but not so misplaced as to invite outright contempt. The gathering of lovers that we find near the conclusion of *As You Like It* perfectly encapsulates such a situation; it is a set-up that the audience knows will be happily resolved. Celia is already promised in marriage to Oliver and it takes little imagination to see that the now-reluctant Phoebe must accept Silvius and that Orlando will marry Rosalind as soon as she throws off her boy's disguise as Ganymede:

PHOEBE: Good shepherd, tell this youth what 'tis to love.
SILVIUS: It is to be all made of sighs and tears,

And so am I for Phoebe.

PHOEBE: And I for Ganymede.

ORLANDO: And I for Rosalind.

ROSALIND: And I for no woman. (5.2.78–83)

The marks of love that are then itemized by Silvius—'to be all made of faith and service'; 'to be all made of fantasy, / All made of passion, and all made of wishes, / All adoration, duty, and observance, / All humbleness, all patience and impatience / All purity, all trial, all obedience'—are felt equally by the other lovers, who sign up to these clichés in all sincerity. Unlike his contemporaries, Shakespeare adds no scorn or social satire to this situation. Oliver, absurdly, gives up his entire inheritance on a love whim, vowing to live with Duke Frederick's daughter in the forest as a shepherd from this point on. The practicalities of such a proposition are not there to be imagined: they run directly contrary to the rules of classical comedy, where getting the girl also means getting the cash. On the stage statements such as Oliver's 'for my father's house and all the revenue that was old Sir Rowland's will I estate upon you, and here live and die a shepherd' (5.2.10–12) are barely registered by the audience; they are merely there to add local colour to a general, wholesome depiction of wild love. This lyrical, soppy mood music is not characteristic of the general run of Renaissance comedy, but it will be familiar to readers in the 21st century from so-called 'chick-flicks' and Valentine's Day cards.

If, in his treatment of wit, Shakespeare looks less modern than we might have expected, the reverse is true of love. Bringing couples together had, from classical times onwards, been a staple of comic plotting and in Italian Renaissance drama the *innamorati* (or lovers) stood at the heart of the play. Yet, on the whole, love in such works involves little real interaction and tends to feel artificial; indeed most classical plays do not depict marriageable virgins on the stage at all. Amongst Shakespeare's English contemporaries these dramatic conventions are also dominant, but in Shakespeare, especially in his middle period, we get something different: sustained, two-way courtship in which the affection of women is taken seriously in spite of the ludicrous confusion that inevitably occurs. This confused courtship lies at the heart of romantic comedy, a modern genre that Shakespeare could be said to invent.

It's complicated

One thing that Shakespeare does to free up his drama is to dissolve the boundaries that normally give such power to the 'blocking' characters in classical comedy. As I observed in the chapter on 'world', the comedies are in fact rarely set in forests, but the lack of a firmly enforced architecture (of specific rooms, lockable doors, or defined settings) means that characters can float free of controlling influences, whether it be those of fathers, dukes, or monarchs. As devotees of children's fiction will know, the first thing you need for adventure to happen is to get parents out of the picture. This is something that Rosalind, Viola, Helena, Beatrice, Portia, and even Isabella (in *Measure for Measure*) achieve early on. One of the things that change when Shakespeare shifts, late in his career, to writing romances (such as *Pericles*, *The Winter's Tale*, and *The Tempest*) rather than straightforward comedies, is that pushy fathers become more prominent in the action and change the mood.

So, without the problem of blocking characters, where does the drama come from? The answer to this question is a very major Shakespearean innovation: relationship trouble. In *Twelfth Night* Orsino loves Olivia, but she is in mourning for her brother and rejects his advances. Viola loves Orsino but ends up being used by him as an emissary to Olivia, who (in spite of her earlier determination to live a life of solitary contemplation) ends up falling in love with what she thinks is a boy. Meanwhile, Sir Toby flirts with the witty Maria, who is socially below him, while encouraging Sir Andrew in his pursuit of Olivia, a countess and somebody well out of his league. Add to this Sebastian, Olivia's identical brother, who also likes Olivia, and the plot begins to run. It is not simply, or even mainly, a matter of confused identities; for all its last minute hysteria *Twelfth Night* is not a farce (for one thing because its geography remains diffuse).

What drives the plot in this play is emotional conflict. Very early on Viola is already aware of the key protagonists' feelings and, having received the gift of a ring from Olivia, sets them out in soliloquy:

> How will this fadge? My master loves her dearly,
> And I, poor monster, fond as much on him,
> And she, mistaken, seems to dote on me.
> What will become of this? (2.1.33–6)

Throughout the play, Viola is a commentator on such split loyalties; in a series of long scenes she converses with Orsino and Olivia, giving an arch but sympathetic commentary on the emotions of all three apparently unrequited lovers. As she says while listening to Olivia's speech of passion, 'I pity you', a half line that is then completed by Olivia with the words 'That's a degree to love' (3.1.123). Just as in other Shakespeare comedies, the frisson of homo eroticism is encouraged through such interactions. The poet works continually to expand the field of possible attraction. Even the foolish and physically awkward Sir Andrew Aguecheek is afforded a rather touching moment of romantic nostalgia when he tells the audience 'I was adored once, too' (2.3.175).

Comparing such moments to the equivalent points in Shakespeare's sources is instructive because it reveals the process of softening and expansion that helps to give the plays a relationship-centred feel. As noted, the plot of a woman in pageboy disguise who is employed by her master to woo a lady who is in fact her love-rival predates Shakespeare. In *Gl' Ingannati* it is Flamminio's discovery that Isabella loves the supposed pageboy he has sent as an emissary that leads to the bloodcurdling threat to 'cut off his lips and his ears and gouge out one of his eyes'. That element of threat is still momentarily there in *Twelfth Night* at the moment of discovery and it's one of the play's troubling aspects, but the way in which the playwright presents it is also markedly different from the situation in his source. In *Gl' Ingannati* the promise of violence is spoken without either Isabella or Leila being present: it is a straightforward expression of intent. In *Twelfth Night*, however, Orsino makes the same sort of threat before an assembled company, with Viola and Olivia (the equivalents of Leila and Isabella) as participants in the dialogue:

> ORSINO [*to Olivia*]: Live you the marble-breasted tyrant still.
> But this your minion, whom I know you love,
> And whom, by heaven I swear, I tender dearly,
> Him will I tear out of that cruel eye
> Where he sits crownèd in his master's spite.
> [*to Viola*] Come, boy, with me. My thoughts are ripe in mischief.
> I'll sacrifice the lamb that I do love
> To spite a raven's heart within a dove.
> VIOLA: And I most jocund, apt, and willingly
> To do you rest a thousand deaths would die. [*Follows Orsino*]
> OLIVIA: Where goes Cesario?
> VIOLA: After him I love
> More than I love these eyes, more than my life. (5.1.122–33)

The threat about eye-gouging in Shakespeare's source haunts this exchange in *Twelfth Night*, even though it is never voiced. Orsino's phrase 'tear out of that cruel eye' (so close to Flamminio's) is only just metaphorical: the threat of violence remains serious, indeed it is made more serious through the biblical overtones of the lamb, Abraham's substitute for his son Isaac as a sacrifice to God. The mood of Shakespeare's scene, however, is very different. What is mere macho rage in *Gl' Ingannati* becomes spiritual and personal. More importantly, in Shakespeare the moment of anger is simultaneously the moment at which love comes to the fore. As at other points in the comedies (for example, the moment where Beatrice confesses her love for Benedick and immediately asks him to 'kill Claudio') the playwright delights in mixed emotions. Orsino himself makes the discovery of his hidden feelings as he shifts from the tentative and euphemistic 'I tender dearly' to the declarative statement about Viola/Cesario 'that I do love'. Shakespeare judges the tone of such moments brilliantly. The love/dove rhyme, which stands out in a passage of blank verse, is the stuff of hackneyed sonnet convention, but by placing it in such an alarming context the playwright gives it a peculiar force. Viola confesses her own love in response to it, weirdly, through a willingness to die.

Does Orsino still love Olivia at this moment? How does he feel, at the same moment, about his love for a young man? The fact that his comedies can prompt such questions sets Shakespeare apart from his contemporaries, whose plays tend to be more clean-lined in their emotional arcs. The so-called 'problem comedies', however we define them, provoke still more speculation. Can Helena in *All's Well That Ends Well* really forgive Bertram? Can this aristocratic playboy learn to love a girl from the wrong side of the tracks? Will Isabella accept the Duke's marriage proposal at the end of *Measure for Measure*? Is Mariana and Angelo in the same play a plausible match? The marriage customs and social mores of Shakespeare's time are radically different from those of the present, so our answers to such questions are bound to be anachronistic. Even so, it is significant that they can be asked. This fact connects Shakespeare with classic romantic comedies of the 20th century such as *When Harry Met Sally*, whose promotional tag line read 'can men and women be friends or does sex always get in the way?'. The quarrelsome couples, wisecracks, and moments of philosophical speculation that we find in Woody Allen movies likewise have their equivalents in the comedies. *Much Ado About Nothing* could be called 'Three Weddings and a Funeral' once the promises of the final act come through. What this shows is that one strain in Shakespearean comedy finds its way into modern cinema. At times, however, the connection goes one step further and the movie-makers go directly to Shakespeare for their source.

A film based on Shakespeare's plot

Successful films of Shakespeare comedies are a comparative rarity, in part because the stage world, with it caricatured action and set-piece dialogues, is so hard to place in a real environment, which the window of the movie theatre almost inevitably displays. Shakespeare's *stories*, however, because they concern relationships, can translate more easily onto the screen. The list of successful films based on the comedies is substantial. Fairly recent examples include *10 Things I Hate About You* (1999), based on *The Taming of the Shrew*; *She's the Man* (2006), based on *Twelfth Night*; and *Get Over It* (2001) and *Were the World Mine* (2008), which are both adaptations of *A Midsummer Night's Dream*. All four of these movies are set, at least substantially, in American high schools: locations with plenty of neutral spaces, a large youthful population, and a set of authority figures whose status can be challenged without genuine anarchy being a threat. The American high school (as an imaginative space) has remarkable similarities to the world of Shakespearean comedy. Also worth noticing, however, are the key points on which Hollywood and Shakespeare take opposite sides.

In *10 Things I Hate About You* Julia Stiles plays Kat, an independent minded grunge-loving feminist teenager at an affluent West Coast day school. The mood of the place is fairly preppy (there is even a club for future MBAs). Kat's sister Bianca, played by Larisa Oleynik, is a prize asset in this environment: she is pretty, rather virginal, and loves designer clothes. Of course Kat is also beautiful, but she has contempt for those around her: in opposition to the dominant jock culture, she likes Sylvia Plath and is applying for a place to study at the left-leaning Sarah Lawrence College. It is easy to see the connections between this environment and the mercantile Padua of Shakespeare's play, where Katherine alone resists the conventions of femininity and courtship, frightening everyone (especially her sister) with her aggressive stance. In the film, Joseph Gordon-Levitt plays a new student at 'Padua High School' who immediately falls in love with Bianca. Like Lucentio in *The Taming of the Shrew,* however, he faces a problem because Bianca's father will not allow Bianca to date unless her 'shrewish' sister also finds a man. The obvious solution is the same as that in Shakespeare's comedy. Gordon-Levitt and another suitor decide to hire a willing third party (Heath Ledger playing the equivalent of the fearless Petruchio) who will court Kat/Katherine while they compete for Bianca's favours on their own terms.

So far, so similar. But what is different? The main thing an audience is likely to remember about Shakespeare's *Shrew* is Katherine's 'taming' by means of Petruchio's wildness: he starves her, denies her clothing, and insists on her slavish acceptance of his authority, no matter how absurd his commands. Even by 16th-century standards this treatment is shocking and the model of wifely obedience on which the play closes was almost as crazy then as it is now. Shakespeare's contemporary John Fletcher actually wrote a sequel, *The Tamer Tamed* (1610), in which Petruchio gets his just deserts. Unsurprisingly, given that the film is targeted at a modern teenage audience, we find no equivalent taming in *10 Things I Hate About You.* Kat becomes nicer, but this is mainly because she realizes that she has hurt Bianca, who herself softens and learns to become more modest about her own charms.

If anything is tamed in *10 Things I Hate About You* it is male bravado. The snobbish MBA bachelor set is humiliated; the vain male model who is Bianca's other suitor (the equivalent of Shakespeare's Hortensio) is exposed and repeatedly punched; and above all the Heath Ledger character (the modern Petruchio) is cured of his antisocial behaviour and taught that dating somebody while secretly being paid for it is a horrible thing to do. The mild peril of a physical female threat to men (what a teacher at the high school calls being 'bitch-slapped') is acceptable; its opposite (men using their physical power over women) is not. In this respect Cole Porter's musical *Kiss Me Kate* (also based on *Shrew*) represents a midpoint in the taming of patriarchy. Here Fred, one half of Cole's warring couple, uses force in response to Lilli as she continues to strike him and she ends up being carried off, hammering her fists on his shoulders (a confrontation that was rendered acceptable to its 1940s audience as a lovers' tiff). In *10 Things I Hate About You*, however, the whole narrative about male control of women is scrapped.

If *10 Things* largely reverses the ethos Shakespeare's original (also including its representation of money) the situation in Andy Fickman's *She's the Man* (see Figure 7) is more difficult to gage. Like its model, *Twelfth Night*, this is a story about a girl who disguises herself as a boy. The film is set in a boarding school called Illyria where Viola passes herself off as her brother (Sebastian) in order to be able to play for the all-male soccer team. Once there she falls in love with the team captain, named Duke Orsino, and inevitable gender confusion follows (especially once Sebastian and the object of Orsino's desire, Olivia, enter the plot). This set-up brilliantly duplicates the situation in Shakespeare: the 'it's complicated' relationship trouble (which was highlighted on the promotional movie poster) shows how much *Twelfth Night* already has of what we might call 'modern love'. Yet, if we look more closely, there are also some major differences that again expose the distance between Elizabethan sensibilities and those of today.

For one thing, *She's the Man* removes the age differential that is important to Shakespeare's original. Shakespeare's Duke is a grown man and Viola is disguised as a teenage boy (or even, according to her initial plan, as a boy eunuch), but in Fickman's film this difference is levelled: the pair are dorm mates of the same age. It is obvious why a modern director would do this: the

7. Promotional poster, *She's the Man* (2006), Dreamworks.

idea of a man using a boy as a love-emissary is, to say the least, sexually suspect, and it becomes still more suspect if there is any suggestion of the man himself falling in love with a boy.

This difference prompts the question: how would an early modern audience have seen the Viola–Orsino relationship? Was it not also awkward for them? It is common to say that because boy actors always played women in Shakespeare's theatre, a Renaissance audience would be blind to such problems, but this is not necessarily the case. Of course, the public attending the Globe were familiar with youths who had a 'feminine' beauty, but this does not mean that they simply 'forgot' that they were boys. There were many contemporary jokes about the sexual attractiveness of such players and when Orsino commends the boy-Viola's lip as 'smooth and rubious' and describes his/her 'small pipe' as like 'the maiden's organ' there is a deliberate play on the womanly qualities of the prepubescent male (1.4.32–3). Although Shakespeare is restrained in such innuendo when compared to most other dramatists of the period, his depiction is still likely to disturb modern audiences, especially in a realist medium such as cinema.

So one thing that *She's the Man* cuts is Shakespeare's depiction of age differential; a second is Shakespeare's depiction of class. The sub-plot of *Twelfth Night* concerns the humbling of Malvolio, the household steward who has the temerity to upbraid his social superiors (such as Sir Toby) and the presumption to woo his mistress, Countess Olivia. In Shakespeare's time cross-class love interest, especially lower class male desire for upper class women, was deeply problematic. The Malvolio plot is still very effective in the theatre: the upstart servant who deludes himself that he is beloved by his mistress, who dresses 'cross-gartered' to attract her, and who pictures himself putting down her relations from a position of power is a wonderful figure of fun. Malvolio's subsequent imprisonment as a madman is a moment of cruelty, but it is still something that a theatre audience can accept. Such a figure, though, is much more difficult to place in a movie because the humiliation of a working man by an aristocrat like Sir Toby is a modern taboo. Again, the director of *She's the Man* makes smart choices. Malcolm (the film's equivalent of Malvolio) is a severely toned-down version of the original: he has no lower class association, he is only mildly humiliated, and there is no intentional plot to bring him down.

So does *She's the Man* show us that today's attitudes are more enlightened? Only to a degree. It is easy to assume that modern ideas about gender are more liberal, but in some respects we are far more absolute about the difference between male and female than was the case in Shakespeare's day. In the early 17th century, young boys and girls were thought of as very similar: before the age of 3 or 4 they were dressed in the same manner and considered medically much alike. Henry Cuff in *The Difference in the Ages of Man's Life* (1607) is entirely typical when he states that the real separation between girls and boys comes around the age of nine, and then only gradually. Today's expectation that boys will be boys from their earliest years (and should wear blue rather than pink to reflect that difference) is a new development. This assumption about an absolute difference between the sexes is very strongly present in *She's the Man*. Viola in the film needs to display a great deal of ingenuity in order to pass herself off as masculine: a 'strut' in the way she walks; a whole aggressive array of laddish humour; and, above all, a lot of experience with the opposite sex. This is very different from the situation in Shakespeare's original, where playing a boy comes quite naturally to a girl. The gap between film and stage here shows the essentialist nature of modern thinking. Today's cinema goers, unlike Shakespeare's original audience, are uncomfortable with the idea that boys really are quite a lot like girls.

We should not fool ourselves, however, that Shakespeare's attitudes are straightforwardly progressive (saying boys are like girls may also imply that women are like children, which is certainly an idea that Orsino entertains). There are limits to the freedom that is granted for personal expression in the comedies and this can be illustrated by one final Shakespeare adaptation for the screen. The 2008 romantic musical fantasy *Were the World Mine* is inspired by *A Midsummer Night's Dream* and is again set largely in a school. In Shakespeare's play Cupid's love potion is used to make Titania fall in love with an oafish mortal and to make the young Athenians, Demetrius and Lysander, fall in love with the same girl. In Gustafson's film, however, the equivalent magic is used to wreak havoc by spreading same-sex desire in a conservative town. The film ends by asking questions about the rights or wrongs of imposing a sexuality on people, questions that Shakespeare could not pose in those terms. There are certainly moments in the comedies that suggest the possibility of homosexual longing: Antonio's love for Bassanio in *The Merchant of Venice*, for example, or Emilia's remembered passion for her friend Flavina in *The Two Noble Kinsmen*. These are, however, temporary states that heterosexual marriage inevitably supplants. In the comedies homosexual identity can never be pressed as a permanent sexual choice.

Thus, though we might say that love in Shakespeare's comedy is more modern than one might have expected, we should also acknowledge that it is more *early modern* than it at first feels. Sex equality in the plays is a fleeting and vulnerable magic, always shut down at the story's end. At that point even Viola must contemplate 'other habits', both of behaviour and of dress (5.1.383).

Chapter 4
Time

The unity of time

Audiences today are likely to be aware of 'the unity of time' as a concept set out by Aristotle. In the *Poetics*, contrasting tragedy with epic, Aristotle states that the former attempts 'so far as possible to keep to the limit of one revolution of the sun or not much more or less, while epic is unfixed in time'. This is a fairly roomy description and Aristotle does not in fact apply it to comedy. Nevertheless, this one-off precept about an entirely different genre did eventually come to exert a strong influence on the construction of comic plays. The *Poetics* was the last of Aristotle's works to be printed in the Renaissance and it took until 1548 for the Italian scholar Francesco Robortello to publish the first major commentary on it. From that point onwards, however, Aristotelian concepts of unity were applied to comic action. The whole thing was taken a step further in 1570 when another Italian, Lodovico Castelvetro (who could be said to have invented the prescriptive 'unities' of time, place, and action) stated that the perfect comedy should be restricted to events lasting no longer than twelve hours.

As a man who moved in intellectual circles, Shakespeare would have been well aware of these prescriptions and he would probably also have known Aelius Donatus's strictures on how the allotted time for a comedy should be divided up. According to Donatus, there were four parts to a good comedy: the prologue, the protasis, the epitasis, and the catastrophe. The prologue was 'the first speech', generally describing the setting and key characters; the protasis was 'the first action' where the story is explained, though with parts held back to arouse suspense; the epitasis complicated the story, intertwining its elements; and finally the catastrophe offered a moment of crisis through which the plot was resolved. The combination of Castelvetro and Donatus thus provided a formula for a faultless comedy.

In *The Comedy of Errors* (1594) Shakespeare makes it clear that he has learnt these lessons. This early work probably had its first performance in front of an audience of Grey's Inn lawyers and for them it must have had scholarly as well as dramatic appeal. The play runs like clockwork. Its opening speech, by the Duke of Ephesus, is a very neat prologue. The Duke pronounces a sentence of death on Egeon, a Syracusian merchant who has illegally entered the bay of Ephesus while their respective cities are at war. Unity of place, time, and action are set down in an instant when Egeon answers (in a statement loaded with dramatic irony) 'my woes end likewise with the evening sun' (1.1.27). Having heard Egeon's backstory (about his lost twin sons with their lost twin slaves and his hopeless search for them) the Duke once more pronounces 'I'll limit thee this day' (1.1.150).

As Shakespeare shifts his play through protasis to epitasis this timeline is rigorously reinforced. Thus, at the beginning of Act 4, we hear that 'at five o'clock' a large sum of money needs to be paid by one of the twin brothers, who remains unaware of his father's plight (4.1.10). By the next scene 'the clock strikes one' and from here on in the pressure is ratcheted up moment by moment until, by start of the final act, 'the dial point's at five' (5.1.119). While the clock itself (as a medieval invention) is an anachronism, it serves a neat classical function, bringing the characters to a temporal crisis that involves all of the entangled plots.

In *The Comedy of Errors* Shakespeare shows himself well capable of following the unities of space, time, and action—even showing off by doubling the difficulties faced in his source text, Plautus's *Menaechmi*, by adding the set of identical twins. Having achieved this, however, Shakespeare clearly felt no pressure to prove the point a second time. A year or two later, when writing *A Midsummer Night's Dream* he did, it is true, offer a version of the unities, but—like everything else in this play—they are a strange, surrealistic alternative to the standard features of classical art. As noted, the play concludes on a curious inversion: a set of 16th-century artisans performing a classical story (that of Pyramus and Thisbe) in front of a mythical Greek hero (Theseus), who clearly existed at a time long before their own. The spirit of classical reversal is also there in its central timeline, which runs not (according to precept) from morning till evening but instead from the evening till the break of day. We do get a kind of protasis and epitasis, and characters such as Puck do feel a sense of time pressure as they anticipate the coming of dawn. Yet the mood of the play is quite the opposite of what we find in *Errors*: it is drowsy rather than mechanistic; instead of desperately asserting their own identity, characters easily shift from one form of being to the next. When, towards the end of Act 4, dawn rouses the lovers, there is no classical catastrophe or revelation; the protagonists just return, somewhat sleepily, to their former selves:

DEMETRIUS: These things seem small and undistinguishable,
Like far-off mountains turnèd into clouds.
HERMIA: Me thinks I see these things with parted eye,
When everything seems double. (4.1.186–9)

Only when the magic of the forest begins to wear off does the absurdity of events become evident to Hermia who, as is characteristic of dreamers, has accepted everything as logical until this point. This progression from acceptance to consciousness about confusion is exactly the opposite of what we expect from a 'correct' classical play.

After *The Comedy of Errors* Shakespeare only follows the unities
in order to expose their absurdity. This, for example, is what we
hear in *The Tempest* (1611) about the play's running time:

PROSPERO: What is the time o'th'day?
ARIEL: Past the mid season.
PROSPERO: At least two glasses. The time 'twixt six and now
                 Must by us both be spent most preciously. (1.2.240–2)

The time from 2 p.m. to 6 p.m. pretty much exactly matches the
maximum running time of plays at Shakespeare's Globe theatre,
so the actor who plays Prospero speaks really about his own time
on the stage. In theory this neat correspondence between 'stage
time' and 'real time in the theatre' should make the play more
believable. Here, however, it actually exposes the artifice of what
the audience sees. *The Tempest* will give its audience flying spirits,
an artificial storm, a disappearing banquet, and a magician (who
to some extent represents the playwright) capable of freezing
men's movements and stopping their speech. Given that this play
sits alongside other late Shakespearean dramas, such as *The
Winter's Tale* and *Pericles*, whose action spans decades as well as
hundreds of miles, the dramatist could hardly have made it clearer
that he intended to overgo the conventional limits of time.

Thinking time

Twelfth Night (1601), in spite of its title, does not have the neat
temporal frame of *A Midsummer Night's Dream*. Nevertheless, it
is tied to a single day. The play is unique in Shakespeare's oeuvre
in referring to a specific point in the calendar: the day of misrule
that marks the end of the Christmas holidays. What is also
unusual about *Twelfth Night* is that record survives of two specific
early performances, both at Candlemas, traditionally the darkest
night of winter, where thoughts turn to the coming of spring.
The play was evidently thought of by its first audiences as
appropriate for moments of transition. They were right to think

this because *Twelfth Night* is very much concerned with the complexities of time.

As was noticed by its earliest reviewer (John Manningham, a fourth-year law student at the Middle Temple in London, who saw *Twelfth Night* on 2 February 1602) the play is 'much like *The Comedy of Errors* or *Menaechmi* in Plautus'. Like both of these earlier plays it has a pair of indistinguishable twins who cause much confusion. In theory, it also has all the time-pressured situations of classical comedy: a gulling plot; fierce competition for a wealthy heiress; a misplaced purse of money; and a citizen from an enemy state who is caught by the authorities and needs urgently to ransom himself. Quite unlike *The Comedy of Errors* or its principal source text, however, this play does not run like clockwork. The more closely we look at the question, the more tangled and elastic the timelines of *Twelfth Night* become.

Already in its opening scenes we get what seems like a superfluous level of detail. The wealthy heiress, Olivia, has made the absurd resolution that the sun 'till seven years' heat / Shall not behold her face at ample view' (1.1.25–6). She, we are told, is in mourning for a father, 'a count / That died some twelvemonth since', and a brother 'who shortly also died' (1.2.32–3, 35). These are very long chronologies to accommodate in a comedy, but they are soon supplemented by others. Characters in *Twelfth Night* continually refer to time. Viola, for example, when we first see her in the Duke's service, has known him 'but three days' (1.4.3). The jester Feste, meanwhile, when he first enters, 'will be hanged for being so long absent' (1.5.15). And Sebastian, Viola's twin brother, reports as fresh news his sister's drowning 'some hour before' he himself was rescued from the waves (2.1.19).

On the face of it, time in *Twelfth Night* feels very specific. Sebastian and Viola's schedules, however, quickly diverge. Like his sister, Sebastian sets off at once for the court of Count Orsino. When he arrives there, however, the shipwreck is—very strangely—'three months' in the past (5.1.91). Just as in *The Comedy of Errors*, references to time increase as the plot thickens, but in *Twelfth Night* they feel impressionistic and wild. This, for example, is how Antonio describes Sebastian's apparent refusal to return his purse:

ANTONIO: [He] grew a twenty years' removed thing
While one would wink, denied me mine own purse,
Which I had recommended to his use
Not half and hour before. (5.1.85–8)

'Twenty years' and the time it takes to 'wink' provide an extreme contrast. Just like the reported 'three months' companionship of Antonio and Sebastian, or the 'three days' that have brought a magical closeness between Orsino and Viola they cannot really be accommodated within the rigid unities. Time in *Twelfth Night* is metaphorical rather than actual. This much is clear from the very unusual stage direction '*clock strikes*', which interrupts the second interview between Viola and Olivia. As Olivia herself observes on that occasion, 'the clock upbraids me with the waste of time' (3.1.129).

It is no wonder that Viola should declare, early on in this drama, that 'time, thou must untangle this, not I' or that Feste should conclude by saying that 'thus the whirligig of time brings his revenges' (2.2.40, 5.1.373). These statements reveal that, while flouting the unities, Shakespeare is intensely conscious of the time-web he is weaving, a web that interlaces the real hours spent on stage and the days and weeks of the plot with a great shaping force that Orsino calls 'golden time' (5.1.378). It is in Feste's song, 'For the Rain it Raineth Every Day', which ends *Twelfth Night*, that we most clearly see that larger perspective. The song is about a daily pattern, but it is also the story of a man's life from boyhood to sleepy death, and in the final stanza it reaches even beyond this:

A great while ago the world begun,
    With hey ho, the wind and the rain,

But that's all one, our play is done,
    And we'll strive to please you every day. (5.1.401–4)

This final stanza starts with the Creation and concludes on the potentially endless cycle of the play's own repetition. It shows the aptness of the work's double title: it is time-specific but it is also '*What You Will*'.

'The unity of time', then, is something much more comprehensive in Shakespeare's middle comedies than simply keeping to the schedule. When Orlando in *As You Like It* states that 'there's no clock in the forest' he is asserting a freedom from normal temporal boundaries, but he is also highlighting a profound thematic interest in the complexities of time (3.2.294–5). Still more so than *Twelfth Night*, this play is filled with references to the hours: 'It is ten o'clock'; 'what is't o'clock?'; 'I come within an hour of my promise'; 'Two o'clock is your hour?'—the list goes on (2.7.22; 3.2.293; 4.1.40–1; 4.1.175–6). According to Rosalind 'time travels in diverse paces with diverse persons' (3.2.301–2) and we see that this is true when we compare the attitude of those around her. Some (notably the jester Touchstone) are continually counting the moments, whereas others (above all the true lover Orlando) are entirely oblivious to the clock.

The dramatist is able to have it both ways. Like *Twelfth Night*, *As You Like It* has conflicting timeframes, for example on the question as to when exactly the old Duke was deposed. The usurpation is still 'news' (albeit 'old news') to Oliver at the play's opening and there are several indications in the dialogue that the 'new' Duke's reign is a relatively recent development (1.1.92–9). Two scenes in, however, the seizure of power is already a distant and hazy memory: 'I was too young that time to value her, / But now I know her' says Celia looking back at the event (1.3.70–1). Repeatedly, Shakespeare plays fast and loose with chronology. Thus, while Rosalind seems to work on a scale of hours, there is time for Oliver to become 'a wretched ragged man, o'ergrown with hair' (1.3.107) and then to recover from this condition over just a few minutes of actual stage time. Twinned with all, there is a subtle seasonal progression—from winter to summer—that is never explicitly stated in *As You Like It*'s plot.

More than anything else, it is the songs that indicate this progression. Songs are a great determiner of mood in Shakespeare's comedies, and *As You Like It* is an exemplary case. There is the brief mention of the 'icy fang' and 'seasons' difference' on the Duke's first entry, but we are not directly told it is winter—that sense is only conveyed by snatches of Amiens' brief ditty 'Here shall he see / No enemy / But winter and rough weather' and his longer song 'Blow, blow, thou winter wind' (2.1.6; 2.5.38–9; 2.7.175). Likewise, the arrival of new growth is conveyed by means of a sprightly song from the Duke's pages, which Touchstone requests from them as soon as he announces that 'tomorrow is the joyful day' of his marriage:

> In spring-time, the only pretty ring-time,
> When birds do sing, hey ding a-ding-a ding,
> Sweet lovers love the spring. (5.3.18–20)

Exile is linked to winter; marriage to spring. Through the songs and a few hints in the dialogue (and, in many productions, changes in scenery) the play takes us from one to the other without ever holding itself to any firm rule of time.

In an influential article first published in the 1940s Northrop Frye argued that 'The Argument of Comedy' was at heart the triumph of fertility over the sterile. This was, he claimed, an older pattern than the boy-gets-girl plot of Greek New Comedy, a tradition of 'folk ritual' that Shakespeare would have encountered as a medieval tradition, but which existed much earlier than that:

> We may call this the drama of the green world, and its theme is
> once again the triumph of life over the waste land, the death and

revival of the year impersonated by figures still human, and once
divine as well.

According to Frye, 'the green world charges the comedies with a
symbolism in which the comic resolution contains a suggestion of
the old ritual pattern of the victory of summer over winter'. Such
symbolism is certainly present in *As You Like It*, which pairs off
an impressive range of couples—Silvius and Phoebe; Oliver
and Celia; Touchstone and Audrey; Rosalind and Orlando—not
so much on the basis of relationships as on the strength of a
seasonal force.

Anne Barton, one of the most brilliant Shakespeare critics, called
As You Like It 'Shakespeare's classical comedy'. By this she did not
mean that it is particularly influenced by the ancients, but instead
that is it archetypal. This play, she argued, 'confers solidity upon
the dazzling experimentation of eight written before it, it stands as
the fullest and most stable realization of Shakespearean comic
form'. This form, she felt, was 'startlingly innovatory' in the subtle
way that it abandoned plot as a fundamental driver and replaced
it with a pastoral stillness, not escapism but rather a natural move
beyond the dictates of time. According to Barton this achievement
was itself time-bound. Shakespeare had worked towards it in the
earlier comedies and he would subsequently 'unbuild' it in the
plays that came after, starting with *Twelfth Night*. In these, she
argued, time increasingly becomes the harbinger of death. Although
this story of personal evolution as an artist has now become less
fashionable, there is something to be said for it. As was argued
by Tony Nuttall (another great critic of Barton's generation)
Shakespeare can be shown to think his way through problems
from one play to another. The evidence for this is especially strong
in the comedies, in which time constitutes an ongoing structural
challenge for the dramatist and also a developing moral arbiter in
the characters' lives. In Rosalind's words, 'Time is the old justice
that examines all such offenders'; where things seem impossible
we must simply 'let Time try' (4.1.189–90).

Long time

According to Barton, Shakespeare immediately began to disrupt the perfect stillness he achieved in *As You Like It* (1600). Certainly by the time we get to *All's Well That Ends Well* (1604-5), the last of the conventional comedies, there is very little stillness to be found. The plot of this play centres on the lowborn Helena, who, as a reward for curing the King of France of an apparently fatal illness, is given the choice of any husband at his court. Helena chooses Count Bertram but he is horrified at the alliance and flees her company. The play then traces her crafty stratagems for securing the man of her dreams. In outline, there is still a progression from winter to summer. The audience is assured that 'time revives us' and that 'time will bring on summer, / When briers shall have leaves as well as thorns' (4.4.34, 31-2). Yet in a world of shady double dealing (where Helena assumes a false identity to trick Bertram, who is a hypocritical womanizer, into sleeping with her) such platitudes carry little weight. 'All's well that ends well yet', the heroine tells us, 'though time seem so adverse, and means unfit' (5.1.27-8). Yet whether all *is* well that ends well is a moot question. Although the play's final scene brings reconciliation, there are arguably just too many dubious acts in recent memory for the short timeline of a stage comedy to fix.

If we use modern genre classifications then Shakespeare gave up writing comedy with *All's Well That Ends Well* around 1605. According to the first Folio, however, *The Tempest* and *The Winter's Tale* are also comedies (and *Pericles*, had it been included in the Folio, must likewise have made it onto that list). Like *All's Well That Ends Well* these late plays depict some shocking acts of betrayal, which conventional comic resolutions would struggle to put right. Yet there is a major difference in the late plays compared to the earlier comedies. The wrongs committed are mended by a gentle influence that can be seen to work miracles: the passage of time.

Pericles, The Winter's Tale (and to some extent also *Cymbeline* and *The Tempest*) are comedies of generational reconciliation that place great emphasis on the passing of the years. In both *Pericles* and *The Winter's Tale* children born in the course of the drama are seen on stage as adults by the play's ending, where they function as a healing force. Shakespeare likes to make the aging of the older generation conspicuous. Thus Pericles has fourteen years of beard growth and in *The Winter's Tale* there is unflattering reference to Hermione's 'much wrinkled' skin, the product of sorrow 'which sixteen winters cannot blow away' (5.3.28, 50). The closing scenes of all four plays present a kind of allegorical tableaux, with age and fertile youth brought together as in classical New Comedy, but with age looking back on errors and misfortunes that stretch a generation back.

It is *The Winter's Tale* that is most explicit about this theme of youth and ageing. The play is the story of Leontes, King of Sicilia, who in a mad fit of jealousy becomes convinced that his wife, Queen Hermione, is unfaithful. His rage has terrible consequences: the loss of his baby daughter, the death of his son, and also (it seems) the death of Hermione herself. Only once these tragedies have happened does Leontes realize his error and he is plunged into a period of mourning that lasts for sixteen years. It is only at the play's close, with his daughter newly rediscovered, that Leontes is invited to come and see a statue, which (it is claimed) depicts his Queen exactly as she would have looked had she continued living. Once he approaches this 'statue', however, it begins to move. The King thus discovers the real Hermione who has kept herself hidden all this while. The reconciliation echoes Claudio's recovery of Hero in *Much Ado About Nothing* (another case of a suspicious lover who is fooled into thinking that he has killed the woman he has wronged). In *The Winter's Tale*, though, the true hurt of false accusation does not pass quickly; only a long period of penance and the arrival of a fresh generation can bring some kind of release.

The ending of *The Winter's Tale*, then, seems to assert that the quick pace of comic resolutions is an illusion: that real men and women take much longer to achieve forgiveness and can never fully return to what they were. Yet in spite of this 'realist' message the conclusion also very much asserts the artifice of the theatre. From the perspective of Leontes it is indeed 'natural' that his Queen should look older. The reverse, however, is true for the audience, for whom her aged appearance is a fabrication created for the stage. This fact is brought conspicuously to our attention when Leontes is warned not to touch the statue because it has just been painted: 'the ruddiness upon her lip is wet. / You'll mar it if you kiss it, stain your own, / With oily painting' (5.3.81–3) he is told. Of course, in the theatre Hermione's lip really *is* wet with oily greasepaint; the audience is reminded that underneath her wrinkled exterior there is the young actor whom we have seen performing less than an hour before. In a way that is characteristic of the late plays, the on-stage characters' avowals of belief in the truth of what they are seeing comes twinned with conspicuous artistic intervention on the playwright's part.

Clocks, seasons, and the process of aging ceaselessly fascinate Shakespeare as comic dramatist. In the comedies the normal laws of time are suspended, even when (as in *The Comedy of Errors* or *A Midsummer Night's Dream*) the author seems constantly to have his eye on the clock. This manipulation of time is an exceptional achievement that sets the comedies apart from other plays.

Chapter 5
Character

Shakespeare's 'round' characters

Shakespeare's ability to create distinct and memorable characters has long been singled out for praise. Alexander Pope, the first to provide extended analysis, declared that 'every single character in Shakespeare is as much an individual as those in life itself; it is impossible to find any two alike'. 'Had all the speeches been printed without the very names of the persons', he added, 'one might have applied them with certainty to every speaker', so distinctive were his modes of speech. Samuel Johnson, a generation later, was scarcely less enthusiastic. In his judgement, 'no poet ever kept his personages more distinct from each other...his scenes are occupied only by men, who act and speak as the reader thinks that he should himself have spoken or acted on the same occasion'.

That Shakespeare should receive such praise for his comic characters is especially remarkable, because comic characters are usually related in some way to fixed types. Yet, according to the Romantic poet, critic, and philosopher Karl Wilhelm Friedrich Schlegel, 'his comic characters are equally true, various, and profound, with his serious', indeed 'so little is he disposed to caricature, that we may rather say many of his traits are almost too nice and delicate for the stage'.

The notion that Shakespeare's characters had a depth that extended beyond their on-stage presence became a Romantic obsession and it ran still more strongly in the Victorian age. The immensely popular biographical critic Edward Dowden, for example, called Portia from *The Merchant of Venice* the supreme example of the 'noble and cultivated woman' and Isabella from *Measure for Measure* an 'immaculate' example of 'heroic chastity' almost as if he knew them as personal friends. The 'inner life' of Shakespeare's protagonists, including his comic ones, became an article of faith.

The logical outcome of this kind of thinking was Mary Cowden Clarke's likewise extremely popular series of books *The Girlhood of Shakspeare's Heroines* (1850–2), a set of novelettes that purported to 'trace the probable antecedents in the history of some of Shakespeare's women' to explain how they had become the women they are. In these we learn, for example, that Viola from *Twelfth Night* was given a virtuous education at the hands of her father who died (as the play indicates) on the twins' thirteenth birthday and 'had a mole upon his brow'. While Viola was growing up her father also made frequent mention of Duke Orsino, which explains her later observation to the Sea Captain: 'Orsino. I have heard my father name him' (1.2.24–5). *The Girlhood of Shakspeare's Heroines* is built on trifles such as these.

It is easy to laugh at Clarke's total faith in the coherence of all Shakespeare's characters. Yet she was, like Dowden, a scholarly reader well versed in the detail of Shakespeare's fiction. The fact that it was possible to construct a whole series of novels out of scraps of information in the play texts is revealing: that same feat would not have been achievable with any other early modern dramatist.

There is something unusual in Shakespeare's methods of characterization, and in fact *particularly* his methods of comic characterization, that gives licence to the fictional biographer's hand. A detail like the mole on the brow of Viola and Sebastian's father is not, in fact, an example of this method. A mole is an entirely conventional feature for a scene of recognition and we find them by the dozen in the sources that Shakespeare used. There are, though, details of a different kind that do not come from his sources and these are key constituents of Shakespeare's distinctive comic art.

It would have been fairly easy for Shakespeare's contemporaries—such as Ben Jonson, George Chapman, John Marston, and Thomas Middleton—to insert 'believable' details into their comedies. The reason that they did not, on the whole, do so was not because of a lack of talent, it was a matter of design. Elite comic writing, especially from the mid-1590s onwards, was concerned above all with 'humours'. These were not 'types' like the 'pantaloon' or the 'zani' of the Italian tradition. The same 'type' could be used repeatedly, but 'humours' were unique creations (or discoveries) that could be used just once. A humoural character has a particular defining obsession, something that has knocked the equilibrium of his or her body (i.e. his or her humours) out of balance. To identify a new comic humour was a significant achievement and doing so had obvious satirical purpose. When Ben Jonson has one of his own characters criticize the play in which he is appearing it is because the author 'has not hit the humours, he does not know 'em' and so cannot capture the exact tone of street life as it exists in London at this time.

To condemn someone like Jonson for creating characters that have no convincing backstory is to fall into an intentional fallacy. His characters are brilliant precisely because they are extremes. The spectacularly greedy Epicure Mammon in *The Alchemist*, for example, is made up almost entirely of ranting speeches about how he will enjoy his money, to the point where even his projected acts of charity ('I shall employ it all in pious uses, / Founding of colleges and grammar schools, / Marrying young virgins…') reveal his hidden desires. The hypocritical puritan Tribulation Wholesome;

the desperate wannabe politician Sir Politic Would-be; the vain courtier Diaphanous Silkworm—these are all examples of Jonson's humours characters for whom one could write no convincing backstory at all.

It was E. M. Forster in his 1927 study *Aspects of the Novel* who memorably divided characters into two categories, 'flat' and 'round'. One of these categories, Forster argued, traced its origins back to the Jacobean age:

> Flat characters were called 'humours' in the seventeenth century, are sometimes called types, and sometimes caricatures. In their purest form, they are constructed round a single idea or quality: when there is more than one factor in them, we get the beginning of the curve towards the round.

When Forster described roundness in opposition to flatness he was talking purely about novels, a form that developed around a century after Shakespeare's death. As is clear from Mary Cowden Clarke's imaginative reconstructions of the youth of Shakespeare's heroines, however, to many observers there is already a novelistic roundness to the characters in Shakespeare's plays.

Jonson worked hard to eliminate contradictions within his comedic characters, making them in one sense as 'flat' as he could, but in Shakespeare it is easy to find individuals in whom 'more than one factor' competes. Even a fairly minor comic creation like Sir Andrew Aguecheek in *Twelfth Night* has several aspects: he is a rich, foolish young gentlemen being exploited by Sir Toby; he is a coward; but he is also rather good company. When we see him, Sir Toby, and Maria together is difficult to see this as pure exploitation because the songs and the jokes they share together create a more complicated sense of fellowship. Jonson might have considered such a character a failure. After all, what is his purpose? He is not really a coherent picture of a failed gallant (such as Jonson created in Fastidius Brisk).

If we were asked what humour he could be purged of, we would be at a loss.

The touches that add roundness to a character like Aguecheek are often just tiny details. For example, in response to Sir Toby's casual boast about being 'adored' by Maria, Sir Andrew responds, briefly and plaintively, 'I was adored once too' (2.3.175). The statement has no consequence in the story and Sir Toby ignores it, but it could be the basis of an entire novella by Mary Cowden Clarke. It the same with the comic constable Dogberry's observation, in *Much Ado About Nothing*, that he is 'a fellow that hath had losses, and one that hath two gowns' (4.2.81–3). Barring a few of these touches, Dogberry could function perfectly well as a satirical portrait of an incompetent policeman, a man grandly in awe of his own office who loves to tell his subordinates what to do. Jonson extracts comedy from similar figures, for instance the Justice of the Peace, Adam Overdo, in *Bartholomew Fair* (1614). But an addition like Dogberry's mention of his 'losses' suddenly adds pathos and suggests a deep and complex backstory. This, along with the superfluous specificity of the 'two gowns' in his wardrobe, give the constable a novelistic aspect that is extremely unusual in Renaissance comedy. Even 'roundish' characters like Volpone in *The Alchemist* do not have such physical oddities to make them human, because Jonson is much more goal-oriented in his character design.

The apparent lack of utility to the comedies was, for a long time, a source of frustration for Shakespeare's critics. 'He seems to write without any moral purpose', wrote Dr Johnson, who was puzzled by a failure that seemed wilful and perverse: 'he omits opportunities of instructing and delighting which the train of his story seems to force upon him'; 'he carries his persons indifferently through right and wrong, and at the close dismisses them without further care'.

The character of Paroles in *All's Well that Ends Well* must especially have annoyed Johnson. Here, finally, is a character who seems to embody a particular vice. His very name signals the fact that he is a talker: a boaster, a liar, a flatterer, a bad-mouther of friends. In the play there is a very Jonsonian plot to cure Paroles of this humour. A group of his fellow soldiers capture and blindfold him, pretending they are the enemy, leaving him terrified. Finally they remove the blindfold, confident that he will now be cured of his humour and 'undone'. In a Jonson play (or in almost any comedy by Chapman, Marston, or Middleton) this would be the great curative moment: purging the character of his defining fault. Paroles, however, observes laconically, 'who cannot be crush'd with a plot?' and resolves to remain unchanged by this humiliation: 'simply the thing I am', he tells the audience, 'shall make me live' (4.3.326–35). Exactly in the way Dr Johnson complained of, Paroles is carried by Shakespeare 'indifferently through right and wrong' and left in an unreformed state at his final exit 'without further care'.

The fact that Shakespeare's characters cannot be tied down to a single function is a potential problem not only for what Johnson calls their 'moral purpose', but also (probably more important from a modern perspective) for their comic effectiveness on the stage. The great comic creations of writers other than Shakespeare are often said to be funny precisely *because* they are so predictable. Bertie Wooster, for example, is reliably dim-witted: he will always be happy at the Drones club, will always make regrettable marriage proposals, and will always try and fail to impose 'the iron hand' on Jeeves. It would spoil our laughter if this character suddenly brought up some painful element in his backstory, like the loss of his parents at an early age. It is Bertie Wooster's mechanical regularity that makes him fun.

The appeal of two-dimensionality in characters is central to one of the great theories of comedy, Henri Bergson's *Le Rire* (1900). According to Bergson's thesis 'we laugh every time a person gives us the impression of being a thing'. Thus, in normal life, people behave in a way that is complex (they might be in love, for example, but when they walk they still remember to look where they are going and can still turn up on time for work). Comedy arises where we strip away those other aspects (the lover cannot walk without bumping into lamp posts and loses all conception of time). Bergson's theory explains why comic movement needs to be stylized and why repetition of a single stylized action (such as bumping into a lamp post) makes us laugh. The theory also states that laughter is opposed to empathy: any fellow feeling for a victim (for example, the belief that bumping into a lamp post might actually hurt them) kills comedy stone dead. We see the truth of these observations when a character such as Dogberry fails to behave like a 'thing' in the way that the law of comedy demands. In the end, Dogberry 'writ down an ass' who 'has had losses' becomes a tragic figure, one whose fate can add a pall of gloom over the conclusion of *Much Ado About Nothing* as a whole.

Shakespeare's most memorable creations—such as Bottom, Falstaff, and Malvolio—tend to have this complicating element of sadness, which can knock comedy off course. Thus, with the exception of the straightforward fun of *As You Like It*, there is always an element of unease. How, then, does Shakespeare combine complexity with laughter? How does he make pathos compatible with farce? One answer is that his characters are shape-shifters. As with stage space, Shakespeare adapts their level of self-awareness to the moment so that, dependent on the requirements of the drama, they can be both 'flat' and 'round'.

Shakespeare's 'flat' characters

Praise for the roundness of Shakespeare's characters is entirely conventional. Appreciation of their occasional flatness, however, is rare. Yet, although the playwright never really produces humoural characters, there are moments where a two-dimensional quality suits him. His lovers, for example, as soon as they start to write sonnets, become resoundingly flat. Rather like Shakespeare's ability to play with time in his plotlines (combining rapid action with much lengthier development in the same frame), there is a striking flexibility in his comic characterization. Some of his characters have an almost cubist aspect, combining the flat with the round.

Shakespeare's ability to flatten his characters without the audience really noticing it in the theatre is especially useful when it comes to denouements. Oliver's switch in *As You Like It* from the fratricidal misanthrope who bullies Orlando in Act 1 to the pastoral lover for Celia in Act 4 is a nice example of this sleight of hand. This could, theoretically, display two factors within his character, but there is so little relation between them and so little is done to explain the turnaround that it makes more sense to say that at both stages his character is simply flat. In a different way, there is strategic flatness in the character of Hermione in the final scene of *The Winter's Tale*. For the first three acts Shakespeare presents her as remarkably eloquent, even strident. In open court she defends herself with both reason and passion against the false accusations of adultery, demands judgment from the oracle, and insists on her status as 'a great king's daughter' who has a right to 'a moiety of the throne' (3.2.38). Yet when, sixteen years later, she reappears as a pretend statue Hermione speaks a very different kind of language—it is mystic, formal, almost entirely stripped of distinctiveness. As with Oliver in *As You Like It* one could, theoretically, come up with a backstory to account for this transformation in Hermione's outlook but this is really not a profitable task. The final act of *The Winter's Tale* is full of strange developments (alongside Hermione's, the actions of Polixines, Paulina, and Leontes are equally difficult to explain). Character, here, must bend with the magic of the fairy-tale ending. Through music, ceremony, and the regularizing of speech patterns Shakespeare does everything he can to flatten out individuality in the denouement of this play.

Relatively speaking, Shakespeare's characters are more consistently flat in his early comedies (*Two Gentlemen of Verona*, *The Comedy*

of Errors, and *The Taming of the Shrew*), which were written
before he became a shareholder in an acting company and was
able to control the casting of his plays. They also flatten towards
the end of his career in the comedies better known as 'romances':
The Winter's Tale, *The Tempest*, and (if one can count them as
comedies) *Pericles* and the joint-authored *Two Noble Kinsmen*.
In the middle comedies (everything from *Love's Labour's Lost*,
composed 1594–5, to *All's Well That Ends Well*, most likely
completed some time between 1604 and 1605) character tends
more often to be 'round'. This outline, though, elides many
complexities, not only because Shakespeare's evolution over time
is more uneven but also because there is huge variation within
plays and within characters.

Some characters lack depth from start to finish. The male
lovers Demetrius and Lysander, for example, remain blankly
interchangeable throughout *A Midsummer Night's Dream*. This
is functional especially in combination with the much more
defined characterization of their female counterparts Helena and
Hermia. The tall, pale, and easily frightened Helena is a deliberate
contrast to the short, dark, and feisty Hermia, and, in their speeches,
they reflect on those qualities as they are by turns adored and
rejected by the men. Their bafflement at the (magically induced)
changing affections of their lovers is made all the more effective
by this contrast between defined and undefined character. Love is
blind, the play tells, and partly this means a man can change
suddenly from loving a tall girl to loving a short one, but it also
means that a woman can hold her passion fixedly on one man
(who hates her) when another (who declares his love for her) looks
and acts just the same.

Some characters, Helena and Hermia for example, stick pretty
fixedly to their round complexity, bearing grudges and remaining
physically distinct. Perhaps Shakespeare's greatest comic
achievement, however, is combining roundness and flatness
within a single character, switching dextrously from the one to the

other, without raising the audience's scepticism, from one scene to the next. The sparring couple of *Much Ado About Nothing*, Beatrice and Benedick, are an example of this flexibility. For the most part, both are witty, cynical, acerbic: by far the smartest couple in the play. Yet, once they are tricked into confessing their love for each other they become clichéd, naive, and brilliantly stupid. Benedick, in particular, switches in an instant into a 'machine' of the kind described by Bergson, as predictable and wooden as a jack-in-the-box. In the theatre the actor playing Benedick must make his actions as stylized as possible: performers in this role regularly fall backwards, stand open-mouthed in amazement, or adopt the pose of the classic lover, hand on heart. Directors often embellish the scene with stage business. Kenneth Branagh, playing Benedick in his own film version, for example, performed a clownish routine with a collapsing deck chair while Edward Bennett, in Christopher Luscombe's 2014 RSC production (under the title *Love's Labour's Won*), depicted Benedick getting entangled in the Christmas tree in which he was hiding, eventually getting frazzled when Don Pedro fixed and turned on the tree's electric fairly lights.

The special brilliance of Beatrice and Benedick as characters lies in this unpredictable movement from roundness to flatness. Uncertainty about depth at any particular moment adds a special frisson to this play in production, notably at the point immediately following the shaming of Hero under a false accusation of unfaithfulness. Here the lovebird two-dimensional version of Beatrice and Benedick suddenly collides with their other rounder, more socially embedded, selves. Audiences generally laugh at the moment where Beatrice answers 'Kill Claudio' (4.1.290) in response to Benedick's love-struck offer to 'do anything' for her, but they do so with nervousness as much as with pleasure. It is a measure of Shakespeare's flexibility of characterization that he can, after this, re-flatten the couple sufficiently for the play's conclusion, where they are exposed for writing 'halting sonnets' full of 'babbling rhyme'.

Round characters in square plots

Normally, Shakespeare is very adept at fitting character to circumstance, giving his protagonists just the right amount of self-awareness to suit their function at that point in the play. Sometimes, however, his tact seems to go missing and here we end up with what the Victorian critic F. S. Boas termed Shakespeare's 'problem plays'. Boas was comparing Shakespeare with Ibsen and included *Hamlet* in his analysis, but the category of drama that he identified came to be applied mainly to comedies. Thus William Lawrence in *Shakespeare's Problem Comedies* (1931) listed *Troilus and Cressida, Measure for Measure,* and *All's Well That Ends Well* as works that 'clearly do not fall into the category of tragedy, and yet are too serious and analytic to fit the commonly accepted conception of comedy'.

Although the category remains a disputed one, Shakespeare's problem plays do have qualities that are distinct from mere tragi-comedies, a Renaissance genre that was championed by the playwright John Marston in the early 17th century, where a midpoint between the tragic and comic is an explicitly identified end. For one thing, the problem plays are about moral problems (such as 'do the ends always justify the means?' or 'does a hypocrite necessarily make a bad judge?'). They are also about social problems, being filled with references to prostitution, political corruption, and sexual disease. Shifting generically between classical comedy, medieval romance, and Renaissance satire, the plays are difficult to categorize at the tonal level. But their biggest problem, one could argue, is the problem of putting round characters into square plots.

By 'square plots' I mean plots that have a strong mechanical regularity: plots that involve substitution, for example, or plots that spell out a very explicit moral lesson. In medieval romance and classical comedy such mechanical regularity is commonplace and, as long as we don't think too much about the practicalities for individuals, the machine that delivers such stories runs smoothly enough. In the problem comedies, however, there is simply too much roundness, too much back-story, for the characters to pass through the mechanism unscathed. Somehow or other, the plot does just about keep running, but there is a noticeable grinding of the gears.

One obvious example of this mechanical regularity is the so-called bed-trick. In both *Measure for Measure* and *All's Well That Ends Well* a man sets up a secret sexual assignation in a dark room with a woman on the basis of a false promise. In *Measure for Measure*, Angelo promises to save Isabella's brother from a sentence of death if she will sleep with him and in *All's Well That Ends Well* Bertram offers Diana 'my house, mine honour, yea my life' (4.2.52) for the same thing. Following some off-stage action both men believe they have got what they wanted, but they betray the bargain: Angelo orders the death of Isabella's brother and Bertram shames Diana as 'a common gamester to the camp' (5.3.191). They are, however, saved from the consequences of their bad actions: first, because the harm they wish to inflict is averted; and, second, because (thanks to a secret substitution) the women that they have slept with are actually their legally intended wives.

Tales of such substitutions crop up regularly in the stage and prose romances that Shakespeare used as his sources. The playwright read versions of the 'monstrous ransom' featured in *Measure for Measure* in numerous dramatic and prose incarnations, both Italian and English, including the earlier play *Promos and Cassandra* (1578) by William Whetstone. The deception practiced on Bertram is likewise found in multiple earlier renditions: folk tales; Boccaccio's *Decameron*; and as 'the thirty-eighth novel' of William Painter's story collection *The Palace of Pleasure* (1575). Though these earlier stories do differ, they also have something in common in that the characters within them are fairly simple in their expressions, thought patterns, and motivation. This, for example, is how Cassandra in *Promos and Cassandra* appeals to the King for her new husband's pardon, in spite of the fact that Promos intended to betray his bargain with her and send an innocent man to a grisly death:

> CASSANDRA: Most gracious King, with these my joy to match
>   Vouchsafe to give my damned husband life.
> KING: If I do so, let him thank thee his wife. [. . .]
> PROMOS: Cassandra, how shall I discharge thy due?
> CASSANDRA: I did but what a wife should do for you.

In a world where people speak like this, it is not so very difficult to believe Promos's response to a final moral homily from the king: 'Most gracious King, I will not fail my best, / In these precepts to follow your behest'.

In Shakespeare's world characters clearly always speak in a more complicated way than in the world of George Whetstone. Yet this is usually not a problem when resolving a comedy, because Shakespeare uses dramatic sleight of hand to cover over something like the ill deeds of Oliver in *As You Like It* or the near-execution of Egeon in *The Comedy of Errors*. In *Measure for Measure* and *All's Well That Ends Well*, however, not only are the ill-deeds of the key characters more egregious, Shakespeare also seems to do everything in his power to make the resolution more awkward and complicated than it needs to be.

The situation of Isabella in *Measure for Measure* is a case in point. Like Cassandra in Whetstone's play, she has a brother who has been condemned to death for having slept with his intended wife before they were legally married. Also, like Cassandra, Isabella is then propositioned by a magistrate (Angelo), who falsely claims he will save her brother in exchange for sex. The fact that Isabella then uses a substitute (Mariana) to sleep with Angelo already complicates matters, but Shakespeare makes things additionally (and unnecessarily) complicated by also making Isabella a novice nun. Shakespeare's Isabella is almost fanatically virginal: she wishes to have a 'more strict restraint' than is fixed for the sisters of the order that she is joining; she describes sex before marriage as the 'vice that most I do abhor', and she feels that her brother has been condemned by a 'just but severe law' (1.4.4; 2.2.31, 41). Her apparent loathing of sexuality sits very awkwardly within the plot's mechanism, in which she receives not only the 'monstrous' offer from Angelo, but also a marriage proposal from Angelo's superior, the Duke.

Isabella is the very opposite of a stock comic character: she is possibly the most idiosyncratic of all Shakespeare's heroines, certainly the most multi-layered figure depicted in the comedies. Cassandra in Whetstone's play is simply a 'very virtuous and beautiful gentlewoman', entirely anodyne, whereas her equivalent in *Measure for Measure* has a set of convictions that are particularly incompatible with the plotting of this story, which involves not only the bed-trick but also a substitution involving a severed head. There are ways of explaining Isabella's actions, but they require pretty deep psychological readings of a kind that we do not normally find in a comedy.

The complexity of Isabella's possible motivation is far from unique in *Measure for Measure*. The Duke, Angelo, Claudio, Lucio—all of these figures in the play have characters that are not simply 'round' but positively lumpy in their many sides and imperfections. Accounts from actors who have played these roles are revealing because they show how very difficult it is to plumb their depths. Roger Allam, for example, who played the Duke in Nicholas Hytner's RSC production of 1987, took a very long time to come to an interpretation that satisfied both him and the director (see Figure 8). The two men found the Duke's speeches 'difficult to understand' because of the 'complex and involved sentence structure' of his speeches in which he 'constantly repeats and qualifies himself, trying to pin down his meaning more precisely'. Added to this, the Duke's actions and his instructions to those

8. Roger Allam as Duke Vincentio proposing to Isabella (Josette Simon) in Nicholas Hytner's production of *Measure for Measure*, RSC (1987), Shakespeare Birthplace Trust.

around him are 'seemingly contradictory'. Duke Vincentio, as Hytner eventually saw him, was a figure in crisis, someone whose 'sense of self has fragmented into "many a thousand grains of dust"'. What Allam's performance tried to show to the audience was the Duke's process of recovery from that crisis and his coming to a new resolution about how he should live his life.

Allam's experience is typical not only of the other actors in Hytner's production but also of those who have performed in other productions of a play that has proved increasingly popular in recent decades. Again and again, actors talk about 'crisis', 'contradiction', 'subconscious motivation', and psychological flaws. This spread of response is unusual for actors in Shakespearian comedy, in which (for all the roundness of its characters) it is generally fairly easy for performers to decide what their characters are thinking, at least on the big questions of love and desire. The 'problem' feel of this comedy, then, comes partly from the sense that the characters have problems within themselves.

The situation in the other 'problem' comedies, *Troilus and Cressida* and *All's Well That Ends Well*, is comparable but also somewhat different. The protagonists here likewise offer potential for psychological interpretation, but alongside this they have a more archetypal quality: at times they feel almost like figures in a fairy tale, half-conscious of their existence in a storybook world. *Troilus and Cressida* is set during the Trojan War (and is thus sourced, ultimately, in Homer's *Iliad*) but its love story is in large part a medieval invention, which Shakespeare knew best from Chaucer's *Troilus and Criseyde*. In different ways, the *Iliad* and *Troilus and Criseyde* are about high and noble people—heroes and heroines, transcendent lovers. Shakespeare's version, however, takes this familiar material and retells it using a cast of painfully ordinary people, characters who are actually in awe of the mythic entities they are supposed to represent.

While trying to persuade each other the characters in *Troilus and Cressida* use clichéd rhetoric (making Helen 'a pearl / Whose price has launched above a thousand ships' (2.2.80–1). Their asides, however, admit to a prosaic reality in which Troilus is 'a sneaking fellow', Hesione simply 'an old aunt', and Cassandra 'our mad sister' (1.2.222; 2.2.76, 97). Again and again the characters stress the absurdity of a situation in which people are created not through their actions but through the words that are used to describe them. Ulysses even walks onto the stage with a book that 'expressly proves' this proposition: 'no man is the lord of anything, / Though in and of him there be much consisting, / Till he communicate his parts to others' (3.3.109–12). Not only does Ulysses insist that nobody is anything without managing to communicate their identity, he also thinks that (like books) people can be endlessly reinterpreted in line with personal preference. For him, Cressida herself is a kind of erotic novel: 'There's language in her eye, her cheek, her lip' and she will 'wide unclasp' herself 'to every ticklish reader' (4.6.56–63). In a world where everyone is using grossly inflated language, this leads to a depressing impasse. Having heard Ajax, amongst others, described as a 'lion', 'bear', and 'elephant' in a single sentence, Cressida poses the inevitable question: 'they that have the voice of lions and the act of hares, are they not monsters?' (1.2.19–20; 3.2.84–6). In the end, what Shakespeare reveals in *Troilus and Cressida* is that no character can be reduced to a singularity, no matter what is demanded of them by the plot. 'This is, and is not, Cressid', says Troilus after he has witnessed her unfaithfulness; and, in the same scene, 'I will not be myself' (5.2.149, 64).

The problem comedies can be seen as the logical outcome of the increasing 'roundness' that Shakespeare brought to his characters. Having started his career creating relatively simple entities, such as Lance in *Two Gentlemen of Verona* or Katherine and Petruchio in *Taming of the Shrew* (both plays composed in the period 1590–1), he moved to brilliantly vibrant masterpieces such as Bottom in *A Midsummer Night's Dream* (1595) and Beatrice and Benedick in *Much Ado About Nothing* (1598). *Twelfth Night* of 1601 is probably the most enjoyable of Shakespeare's compositions when it comes to diversity and depth of comic characterization: the love-sick Orsino; the feeble Sir Andrew Aguecheek; the pompous Malvolio; the riddling and satirical Feste; the drunken Sir Toby Belch; the list goes on—there is hardly a forgettable character in the play. After 1601, however, we get *Troilus and Cressida* (1602), *Measure for Measure* (1603), and *All's Well That Ends Well* (1604–5). Diversity and depth, here, are greater than ever, but they are no longer easily enjoyed. Partly, this is because the subject matter of these plays is more serious, but it is also because the characters now have so many different factors in them that they cannot be accommodated, as Shakespeare's characters were previously, into the mechanism of a comic plot.

After he finished *All's Well That Ends Well* Shakespeare concentrated for a while on tragedies such as *King Lear* and *Macbeth* (of 1605–6) in which characters seem to have profound and troubled psychological depths. This troubled quality in Shakespeare's characters does connect the problem comedies to the later tragedies. Perhaps the playwright simply became too interested in the darker aspects of human motivation to continue with comic writing in his old way? Certainly, roundness of character had always stood in potential opposition to laughter. Keeping the two in balance was no easy trick. If Shakespeare sometimes struggled with this equation, however, that struggle was ultimately productive. The complexity and life of his characters (the way they stand in consistent, meaningful relation to each other) is exceptional across the comedies: along with unique qualities of space and time in Shakespeare's dramaturgy it is the unusual complexity of his characterization that stands out.

Endings

The end of comedy?

After *All's Well That Ends Well* (1604–5) Shakespeare put the writing of comedies aside and wrote four tragedies in succession: *King Lear* (1605–6), *Macbeth* (1606), *Antony and Cleopatra* (1606), and *Timon of Athens* (1605–7). Hereafter, *Pericles* of 1607 could be called a comedy on grounds of its happy ending. The Quarto edition refers to 'the whole history, adventures, and fortunes of the said prince' but makes no real attempt to define its genre, and, as it was not included in the 1623 Folio, it is hard to know how the actors would have classified this play. Whatever we label it, however, *Pericles* has few laugh-out-loud moments and audiences today are most likely to think of it as a romance.

So did Shakespeare write any comic plays after *All's Well That Ends Well*? The editors of the Folio listed both *The Winter's Tale* (1609–10) and *The Tempest* (1611) as comedies, but, as with *Pericles*, modern criticism has tended to think of these works as romances—in production they feel much more dreamy than mainstream comedies like *As You Like It* (1600) or *Twelfth Night* (1601). The conventional story, therefore, has been that comedy, for the playwright, came to an end pretty early in the 17th century, even though he had almost a decade of writing for the theatre still to come. If we accept that this is what happened, what factors can we put forward by way of explanation? For example, did theatrical fashions change to make comedy less marketable? Or was serious, psychological tragedy suddenly in vogue?

Of course, Shakespeare, as a commercial playwright, was always at some level responding to the work of his rivals. The move away from comedy, however, was not a general trend at this time. Between 1604 and 1605 there was, for example, strong demand for city comedies. *Westward Ho* (1604), written by Dekker and Webster, was quickly followed by a rival commission: *Eastward Ho* (1605) from the team of Chapman, Jonson, and Marston. Dekker and Webster's response with *Northward Ho* (1605) did not take long. Shakespeare's *King Lear*, written in the same period, looks like an outlier—nobody else was writing this kind of tragedy at this time. The following year, Shakespeare's own company performed Ben Jonson's brilliantly funny *Volpone* (1606), which competed with numerous other strong comedies, including Thomas Middleton's *The Puritan* (1606). Again, Shakespeare's contribution, *Macbeth*, bucks the trend in the market—though there were certainly plenty of other tragedies, none has the kind of intense spiritual focus we find in Shakespeare's play.

If it was not fashion, another possible explanation for the abandonment of comedy could be personal. For a long time it was very popular to read Shakespeare's development in this way. The first to propose this line of argument was Edward Dowden in his immensely successful and oft-reprinted book *Shakspere: A Critical Study of His Mind and Art* (1875). For Dowden there was a straight correspondence between the mood of the plays and the inner state of the artist. The comedies written at the start of the new century were thus the moment where Shakespeare 'yielded his imagination and his heart to the brightest and most exuberant enjoyment', but they were followed by a spiritual crisis that made its mark in *Hamlet*, *Othello*, *Lear*, and *Macbeth*. The 'strange and difficult' *Troilus and Cressida*, wrote Dowden, 'was a last attempt to continue comedy made when Shakspere [*sic*] had ceased to be able to smile genially' and was beginning his struggle to retain 'sanity and self-control'.

Beyond the plays and the *Sonnets* (published 1609) there is no evidence to support Dowden's speculation, but this pattern of reading the drama as a clue to the inner life remains seductive. Even today, almost all Shakespeare biographers give way to it to a certain extent and many carry it to still further extremes. The idea of reading any early modern fiction as a confessional statement is, however, potentially anachronistic: even poetry in this period rarely involves direct self-expression; still less do we find it on the public stage. Are we to believe that Shakespeare was feeling bloodthirsty when he wrote *Titus Andronicus*, with all its grisly amputations, and then recovered his 'sanity and self-control' to produce *The Comedy of Errors* a few months further on? In the likeliest chronological order the crisis-filled *Hamlet* sits neatly wedged between the joyous *As You Like It* and *Twelfth Night*; there is no good reason to suppose that Shakespeare flitted from happiness to crisis and then back to happiness during this time.

This is not to say that Shakespeare's writing was unaffected by external factors; the best modern criticism, however, tends to trace more practical influences (such as the decisions of patrons, developments in playhouse design, or changes in the acting company's membership) rather than imagining the inner life of the poet without having access to any biographical texts. If we want to account for the dropping away of comic writing by Shakespeare after 1603 there are various explanations of this practical kind that deserve consideration. For one thing, after 1603 Shakespeare had the monarch as a personal patron. James I gave the company the privilege of calling themselves The King's Men and the plays that Shakespeare wrote immediately after the conferral of this honour spoke directly to the head of state's interests. *Lear* was about the unity of the Kingdom (as the monarch sought to unite England and Scotland); *Macbeth* was set in the King's native country and concerned his pet topic, witchcraft; *Antony and Cleopatra* was about empire and statecraft. All these plays would have appealed directly to the King, whereas the old Histories, with their English focus and their occasional negativity about the Scots, were unlikely to get a good reception from the new regime. With a back catalogue of comedies that the King was very happy to watch (having missed them in their first productions), it made sense for Shakespeare to concentrate his energies on serious plays that would demonstrate his dedication to the court.

To switch temporarily to tragedy also fitted with the interests of Shakespeare's most important collaborator: his lead actor Richard Burbage. Although Burbage could certainly do comedy, his passion was for serious plays and it was for the tragic roles of Hamlet, Lear, and Othello that he would be remembered at the time of his death. In 1599 Shakespeare invested heavily in the new Globe playhouse, a theatre in which Richard and his brother Cuthbert Burbage had a controlling 50 per cent stake. The dramatist's interests and those of Richard Burbage were now closely aligned. Burbage, who was getting on in age, wanted major tragic roles with which to impress his public. The departure of the clown Will Kemp in 1600 was yet another factor because his replacement, Robert Armin, specialized in a kind of comedy that also fitted into tragic plays (most obviously as the character of the Fool in *King Lear*). That Shakespeare's production of comedies should slacken off under these conditions is hardly a surprise.

The twin influence of King James and Richard Burbage does much to explain why Shakespeare put comic writing to one side after *All's Well That Ends Well*. That influence, along with Armin's, can probably also account, at least in part, for the more sombre mood of the so-called problem plays. Shakespeare's most important patron and lead actors alike were pushing for darker, more morally weighty work. It would be a mistake, however, to conclude that Shakespeare's break with comedy was either fundamental or permanent. Even his most serious plays are touched by the comic. Still more important: there would be a late and vital flowering of comedy in the final stage of Shakespeare's career.

Tragical-comical-historical

In the Folio text of *Hamlet* the longwinded courtier Polonius gives the following introduction to the players who have come to visit the castle of Elsinore:

> The best actors in the world, either for tragedy, comedy, history, pastoral, pastoral-comical, historical-pastoral, tragical-historical, tragical-comical-historical-pastoral, scene individable or poem unlimited. Seneca cannot be too heavy nor Plautus too light for the law of wit and the liberty. These are the only men. (Folio text 2.2.394–400)

As with everything that Polonius says, there is a bit of wisdom as well as a great deal of absurdity in this description of early modern genre, because if one wanted a classification of the kinds of plays available in Shakespeare's theatre one would come out with just such a compound list. The play in which this character appears is itself an example. For although *Hamlet* is perhaps the quintessential tragedy, the play nevertheless absorbs many other genres within it, including the tragical-historical morality of *The Murder of Gonzago* and the classical epic of the 'rugged Pyrrhus' speech, both of which are performed by the visiting players. Comedy too is part of this mixture. Polonius is a classic Pantaloon from the *Commedia dell'arte*, while Prince Hamlet is frequently clownish and he has been compared by critics to the anarchic medieval figure of the Vice.

Shakespeare is endlessly inventive in his generic hybridization. The label tragical-comical-historical-pastoral, for example, could be attached to the English Histories, especially to *Henry IV Part II*, in which the scenes set in rural Gloucestershire are amongst the funniest and saddest that Shakespeare wrote. Sir John Falstaff, who stars in these exchanges, defies classification. He is, according to his own definition, 'not only witty in myself, but the cause that wit is in other men' (1,2,9–10). This makes him a brilliantly satirical commentator and also the centre-point of a great deal of physical comedy, yet beyond this there is tragedy in his make-up, something encapsulated in his eventual rejection by Hal when the prince takes on the mantle of King. As depicted by Antony Sher in Gregory Doran's 2014 RSC production of the Henry IV plays, Falstaff was a genuine alcoholic: a desperately self-destructive individual full of hidden anxiety and pain. At the same time, the fat knight is a carnival creation, the embodiment of mirth. Through this combination of extremes, Falstaff shows how reductive it is to parcel up Shakespeare's output into 'comedies', 'histories', and 'tragedies', however useful this may be for a set of Oxford VSIs.

In her superb critical study, *The Comic Matrix of Shakespeare's Tragedies* (1979), Susan Snyder argues that *Romeo and Juliet*, *Hamlet*, *Othello*, and *King Lear* are all dependent on the conventions and assumptions of comedy, not because they have funny moments (though they all do so) but because they actually use comic structures in their core design. *Romeo and Juliet* (1595), in her assessment, starts out as a comedy of love and then turns rapidly and unexpectedly towards a tragic outcome. Its world of bawdy servants, young lovers, and oppositional parents set in small town Italy is traditionally comic: judging from its opening scenes we might expect this play to end in marriage rather than death.

Othello (1603–4), likewise, deploys these comic structures and conventions, and then twists them towards a tragic end. By way of comparison, George Chapman's *May-Day*, which was performed in the same period as *Othello*, is also set in Venice, has almost exactly the same plot set-up of suspected infidelity, and a very similar cast of characters (including a soldier who leaves to fight for the city, a wife who is pursued by a Roderigo-like suitor, and a duplicitous friend). This play, however, ends in laughter and forgiveness, rather than the murder of an innocent wife. Othello is in certain structural ways a 'comic' character: he lacks self-knowledge, he thinks himself a cuckold, and he is tricked by simple gulling devices such as the trick of the stolen handkerchief or the overheard conversation between Iago and Cassio, which Othello misapplies to his wife. The neoclassical critic Thomas Rymer fulminated about these things in his *Short View of Tragedy* (1693) because—according to the traditional theories (those propounded by Donatus, Robortello, and Castelvetro)—subjects like marriage, infidelity, low-class characters, and mix-ups about handkerchiefs, all belonged in the realm of comedy: it was absurd to put them in a play with such a bloody end. Shakespeare and his original audience, however, were not ignorant of these traditional theories, they were simply more open to experimentation. For an audience at the Globe on the Bankside it was exiting to see a playwright take the outline of a play like Chapman's *May-Day* and then combine it with a radically different contemporary genre, in this case Domestic Tragedy (which was often based on sensational real life trial reports), to produce a shockingly different effect.

King Lear (1605–6) is the most extreme of Shakespeare's experiments with comedy inside a different genre. Here we have not only the Fool's caustic humour and the madcap gibberish of Edgar as Poor Tom, but also the absurd spectacle of Gloucester in his blindness being tricked into believing that he has survived his leap from the great height of Dover Cliff. Performed on a bare flat stage, the lead-up to Gloucester's attempted suicide is full of comic potential as the disguised Edgar leads his father and tries to maintain the illusion that they are climbing:

EDGAR: You do climb up it now. Look how we labour.
GLOUCESTER: Methinks the ground is even.
EDGAR: Horrible steep.
             Hark, do you hear the sea?

GLOUCESTER:	No, truly.
EDGAR:	Why, then, your other senses grow imperfect
	By your eyes' anguish.
GLOUCESTER:	So may it be indeed.
	Methinks thy voice is altered, and thou speak'st
	With better phrase and matter than thou didst.
EDGAR:	You're much deceived. In nothing am I changed
	But in my garments.
GLOUCESTER:	Methinks you're better spoken. (4.5.2–10)

An actor with a good sense of comic timing can make Edgar's replies increasingly absurd here as the deception threatens to collapse. His old father's deadpan replies can likewise bring the house down, but the exchanges are no less full of sadness for that. At such moments Shakespeare's use of laughter actually heightens the sense of suffering, as it can in the much later plays of Bertolt Brecht or Samuel Beckett. In Susan Snyder's analysis the 'comic parenthesis' of what she calls Gloucester's 'pratfall' gives the audience 'not just the spectacle of absurdity but an experience of it'. Overall, she argues, *Lear* involves the 'most radical use yet of comedy in tragedy' because Shakespeare 'sets comic order side by side with comic chaos, and out of the dislocation that results he develops a special, devastating tragic effect'.

The non-dramatic verse likewise conjoins comic feelings with other emotions, especially when exploring the absurdities of sexual desire. *Venus and Adonis* (1592–3) thus revels in the mismatch of its title characters, a huge lustful goddess and a diminutive reluctant boy. Venus bullies the object of her desire from the beginning, plucking Adonis from his horse and carrying him off under her arm. This is the first of a series of ridiculous mental images that Shakespeare presents of the couple: later, Venus actually keeps Adonis locked tight within the circle of her arms. The language of erotic persuasion, traditionally used by men in relation to women, is distorted to the point of parody in this context as the love deity presents an inflated blazon of her own charms:

'Fondling,' she saith, 'since I have hemmed thee here
Within the circuit of this ivory pale,
I'll be a park, and thou shalt be my deer.
Feed where thou wilt, on mountain or in dale;
    Graze on my lips, and if those hills be dry,
    Stray lower, where the pleasant fountains lie.' (ll. 229–33)

Bad puns proliferate in this misapplied rhetoric: 'pale' describes Venus's ivory fingers but also the fence that those fingers build around the boy—in her fantasy her 'dear' becomes almost literally a deer. After this comes a wave of *double entendres*: 'sweet bottom-grass', 'found rising hillocks', and the like. Even as Adonis dies and is mourned by the goddess these comic games with language continue, provoking wry laughter amidst the gentle melancholy of the story itself. In a more tempered way that same playfulness and wit is there in the *Sonnets* (published 1609), most obviously in the anti-Petrarchan lyric of 'My mistress' eyes are nothing like the sun' (130, l. 1). Just as with the tragedies, the darkest of the sonnets also deploy a sour humour to express alienation, as with the bawdy puns on 'Will' in sonnets 134 and 135. Comedy, for Shakespeare, is thus frequently a way of increasing the intensity of tragic or erotic experience—something far more complex than the traditional notion of 'light relief'.

There are, of course, also 'comedies' that veer close to tragedy: the humiliation of Katherine in *The Taming of the Shrew* might be read in this manner, as might the crushing of Shylock in *The Merchant of Venice*. The plot of the comedy *Much Ado About Nothing* has much in common with the tragedy *Othello*. And, as we have seen, the 'problem comedies' of *Measure for Measure*, *All's Well That Ends Well*, and *Troilus and Cressida* are full of dark thoughts about human failings and end on resolutions that are deeply compromised. Thus, while 'comedy' is a useful workaday label, it ultimately hides as much as it reveals.

As far as the Folio contents page goes, the category of 'comedy' is a pretty crude one: plays that end in marriage are comedies, whereas the tragedies (with the partial exception of *Cymbeline*) all end in death. *Love's Labour's Lost*, admittedly, 'does not end like an old play', but it does promise a reconciliation between the various couples after a twelve-month wait. None of the Histories or Tragedies have this resolution (even if *Henry V*, with the wooing of Princess Katherine, gets close).

When it comes to plot and content summary, the Folio contents page has its uses. Its categories of 'Comedy', 'History', and 'Tragedy', however, are much more helpful to criticism if they are understood not as ways of defining plays in their entirety, but rather as elements that we can see in operation *within* each individual work. In this context, 'comedy' can be defined as a set of conventions, attitudes, character-types, and pre-existing plot-structures, which may or may not be funny at a particular time. Things like embarrassing physicality, an extreme lack of self-awareness, or conclusion on marriage may in this sense be elements of comedy, even if they occasion terrible and tragic pain. For all his pedantry, Polonius with his category of the 'tragical-comical-historical-pastoral' appears to understand this. Shakespeare, with his brilliant ability to fuse genres, certainly did.

The late comedies

One reasonable answer to the question 'did Shakespeare stop writing comedy after *All's Well That Ends Well*?' would be 'no, because comedy continued as a key element in the tragedies that he wrote after completing that play'. That answer, though, would still imply that Shakespeare stopped writing *comedies* as a genre, and this—arguably—would also be a mistake.

As has already been noted, *The Winter's Tale* (1609–10) and *The Tempest* (1611) are listed as comedies on the contents page of the Folio. Although critics have been sceptical about that classification there are good reasons to accept it. Not only do both plays end in reconciliation and the prospect of marriage, they also contain a good deal of clowning. *The Winter's Tale* has the trickster Autolycus and *The Tempest* has Trinculo the jester, both highly distinctive comic characters that were almost certainly performed by the actor-comedian Robert Armin. In combination with various country clowns, a drunken butler, and the 'monster' Caliban, they produce a good deal of knockabout stuff. While *Pericles* (1607) is, it is true, filled with 'painful adventures', it does feature a set of joking fishermen, has a substantial amount of music and dancing, and concludes with a happy marriage.

There are, then, quite a few candidates for the title of 'comedy' that are written by Shakespeare after *All's Well That Ends Well*. If we look beyond *The Tempest*, moreover, then *Cardenio* (1613) and *The Two Noble Kinsmen* (1613–14) also enter the frame. All five of the late works could also be called 'romances', but romance (like pastoral or lyric) is a mode that Shakespeare makes use of throughout his writing rather than, strictly speaking, being a dramatic genre in its own right. If we abandon romance as an exclusive category, it becomes possible to recognize Shakespeare's 'late comedies' as the final phase of a long and complex exploration—stretching over at least seventeen plays and nearly two and a half decades—of dramatic plots with a happy end.

Pericles, *Cardenio*, and *The Two Noble Kinsmen*, it should be acknowledged, are not exclusively Shakespearean creations. The first, at least in the version that came to be printed, seems to have been written in significant part by an unsavoury character called George Wilkins. Possibly Wilkins got hold of part of a legitimate Shakespeare text and then padded it out (writing most of acts one and two) for pirate publication; or possibly the two men actively collaborated on the play. What is certain is that *Pericles*, as it comes down to us, is unreliable textually: an editor needs to intervene a good deal to get the Quarto to make sense. *The Two Noble Kinsmen* is a pretty good text and its title page is quite explicit about its co-authored status: Shakespeare wrote it together with John Fletcher towards the end of his career. *Cardenio* is absolutely unreliable as a text and quite possibly not a word of the play as it was printed in 1728 was written by Shakespeare. Still, there was a play called *Cardenio*, which was almost certainly written by Shakespeare and Fletcher, and, from tracking down the source of this story in Cervantes's *Don Quixote*, we can make reasonable deductions about its plot.

Pericles, *Cardenio*, and *The Two Noble Kinsmen* all end on at least one marriage, and *Cardenio*, in the version that was printed in the 18th century as *Double Falsehood, or, The Distressed Lovers*, ends as follows:

> DUKE: Your sev'ral nuptials shall approve my joy,
>   And make griev'd lovers that your story read
>   Wish true love's wand'rings may like yours succeed.
>   (5.2.280–2)

As an ending, this has much in common with *The Winter's Tale* and a fair bit with *Pericles*. Indeed, in this company, apart from the fact that the newlyweds Imogen and Posthumous start the play already married, one might reasonably claim *Cymbeline* as a comedy as well.

So if we accept these five or even six late plays as comedies, what does this tell us about the way that Shakespeare expanded the genre in the final stage of his career? For one thing, he extended comedy's geographic and temporal reach, making this traditionally compact form span nations and even continents and taking his protagonists from their youth to their old age. In both *Pericles* and *The Winter's Tale* characters are tracked from their birth to their marriage, as well as from one country to another, between the beginning and the end of the play.

On top of this expansion and elongation, Shakespeare (in the late plays) heightened the element of plot surprise, more often keeping the audience in the dark about key facts. At the end of *The Winter's Tale*, for example, the audience knows no more than does Leontes that his queen, Hermione, is alive and has been living in hiding with Paulina for sixteen years. With this surprise, there also came an increased element of jeopardy, sometimes even bringing in deaths, such as those of Leontes's son Mamillius and Paulina's husband Antigonus (who famously exits 'pursued by a bear'). All of these developments, however, could still be fitted within an essentially comic frame. As is suggested in the echo in its title, even Shakespeare's last work, *The Two Noble Kinsmen*, still has a good deal in common with his first, *The Two Gentlemen of Verona*. Both plays are based on a comic mainstay (the theme of two good friends who are turned by love into fierce rivals); either could be called a comedy as well as a romance.

The plot of the rival lovers is just one example of the wider use of archetypal comic structures in the late plays. The reconciliation of the older and younger generation had, for example, since Greek New Comedy, been a standard feature of the genre. This had traditionally been done through the 'blocking' father figure's acceptance that he had been thwarted: that his son or daughter was going to get married in spite of an old man's regrets. Characters from Baptista in *Taming of the Shrew* to Egeus in *A Midsummer Night's Dream* are Shakespearean examples of this type. In his late plays Shakespeare is playing games with this well-known pattern in comedy. *The Tempest*, for example, features Prospero playing the stern blocking father. He tells Miranda that her lover Ferdinand is unworthy of her and he rages at the young man who has designs on his daughter with just the same wildness as any miser in a *comedia* plot:

PROSPERO: I'll manacle thy neck and feet together.
Sea-water shalt thou drink; thy food shall be
The fresh-brook mussels, withered roots, and husks
Wherein the acorn cradled. Follow! (1.2.464–7)

The twist in *The Tempest* is that the old man is actually a
match maker for his daughter, whetting the young lovers'
appetites by raising obstacles, 'lest too light winning / Make the
prize light' (1.2.153–4). Prospero choreographs their union with all
the precision of a classical theorist, orchestrating the reconciliation
of old enemies plus the defeat of a clownish rebellion, as has
already been noted, in the 'time 'twixt six and now' (1.2.241).

The Tempest is full of the snippets of comic devices rearranged
in a new pattern and this is more widely true of the plays
Shakespeare was writing in this period. *The Winter's Tale* also
mucks around with the old conflict of generations: here it is an old
couple rather than the young one that takes centre stage at the
climax, the young Florizel and Perdita (already married) looking
silently on. In the same vein, the play rehearses and transforms
the escape into a greenworld we find in *As You Like It*, because
here Autolycus (a court-raised trickster played by Armin, the same
actor who played Touchstone) is defeated by country clowns who
turn out to have been closer to royalty than he. *The Two Noble
Kinsmen*, meanwhile, revisits the Athenian wood that is the
setting of *A Midsummer Night's Dream*, where Duke Theseus and
Hippolyta (who marry in Act 1 of *The Two Noble Kinsmen*) still
rule. Just as in *A Midsummer Night's Dream*, in *The Two Noble
Kinsmen* multiple characters pursue the same love-object, not just
the kinsmen themselves (Palamon and Arcite in love with Emilia)
but also a jailor's daughter, in love with Palamon, and an
unnamed wooer, who is in unrequited love with her. The play even
has a version of Peter Quince and the rude mechanicals, with a
schoolmaster and a troupe of country folk rehearsing in the wood
to produce an entertainment for the Duke and his bride. Such
connections demonstrate a continuity between the late plays and

the earlier comedies, making them part of an internal dialogue in Shakespeare's oeuvre that ran for two and a half decades of theatrical experiment.

Had the surviving actors of Shakespeare's company who published the 1623 Folio got hold of good texts of *Pericles*, *Cardenio*, and *The Two Noble Kinsmen* they would logically have listed them amongst the comedies and this genre would then have taken up an entire half side of the book's contents page. In such a case it would have been evident from the outset that Shakespeare not only began and ended his career by writing comedies but that comedies had always been the dominant form in his art. Had he lived beyond the age of 52, who knows what further comic innovations he might have developed? If we had better texts of these late plays we would have a clearer picture, but the good texts of *The Winter's Tale* and *The Tempest* already show that Shakespeare's interest in comedy was becoming still broader, blending laughter with a sense of magic in an immersive musical experience that combined dramatic revelation with a real sense of threat. Following on from the so-called 'problem comedies' written at the turn of the century and the 'festive comedies' that preceded them, these late plays can be seen as simply the last of a long series of experiments determining what can be done with a plot that ends on marriage.

Shakespeare stands out amongst his contemporaries for his unique success across the three basic genres of the Early Modern Theatre—comedy, history, and tragedy—but, numerically at least, there can be no doubt about his favourite. Shakespeare was, first and foremost, a comic poet. In other genres too, he is notable for bringing in comic material, from the gravediggers in *Hamlet* to the clown in *Antony and Cleopatra*, from Falstaff in the *Henry IV* plays to the Fool in *King Lear*. It was this apparently careless slippage into laughter that made Dr Johnson conclude that 'his tragedy seems to be skill, his comedy to be instinct' and that 'in his comic scenes he seems to produce without labour what no labour can improve'. Johnson's words are a testament to Shakespeare's achievement: part of the joy of the comedies is an easeful, purposeless quality that no other dramatist has been able to match. It would be a mistake, however, to assume that this effect of effortlessness came without effort; while we have no evidence of how the playwright felt as he was composing, there is, without question, enormous intellectual energy in his comic work.

The history of Shakespeare's comedies is one of constant innovation. He goes from hard-edged classical plots like *The Taming of the Shrew* (1590–1) and *The Comedy of Errors* (1594) to lyrical and intellectual compositions such as *Love's Labour's Lost* (1594–95) and *A Midsummer Night's Dream* (1595). A few years later, after the mercantile calculating world of *The Merchant of Venice* (1596–7) and *The Merry Wives of Windsor* (1597–8), come festive, escapist locales such as the forest in *As You Like It* (1599–1600) and the poetic Illyria of *Twelfth Night* (1601). Then, late on, following the corrupt, claustrophobic courts found in problem plays like *Measure for Measure* (1603) or *All's Well That Ends Well* (1604–5) comes the unbounded make-believe of *The Winter's Tale* (1609–10), *The Tempest* (1611), and the final collaborative plays. What is evident even from this brief overview is that Shakespeare kept thinking about comedy: pushing what he could do with it, never content to repeat what had already been done. For him comedy was not a stable entity. Comic plays could be punitive or all-forgiving, lugubrious or festive, tightly plotted or almost without any storyline at all. Yet, in spite of this, there is a family likeness across this diverse output, an elusive 'Shakespearean' continuity that this Very Short Introduction has tried to pin down. A shared quality of space, wit, love, time, and character is evident across these dramas, from the first, which was composed around 1590, to the last, which was completed in 1614.

References

All Shakespeare quotations, unless otherwise stated in the notes below, are taken from Stanley Wells and Gary Taylor, eds, *Works*, 2nd edition (Oxford: Oxford University Press, 2005) and appear in the text.

Chronology

For the evidence underlying this compositional chronology, see Bart van Es, *Shakespeare in Company* (Oxford: Oxford University Press, 2013), 312–14. I date *As You Like It* as 1600 rather than 1599–1600 (the date range set out in Stanley Wells and Gary Taylor, *William Shakespeare: A Textual Companion* (Oxford: Oxford University Press, 1987)) because I believe its fool, Touchstone, could only have been written for Armin, who joined the company after the Lent of that year.

Introduction

Donatus, 'On Comedy' translated in O. B. Hardison Jr et al., ed., *Medieval Literary Criticism* (New York: Frederick Ungar Publishing, 1974), 39–49 (45).

Harley Granville-Barker, *Prefaces to Shakespeare*, first series (London: Sidgwick & Jackson, 1927; repr. 1949), 19.

Chapter 1: World

John Dryden, *An Essay of Dramatic Poesy* (1668) in *Works* ed. Keith Walker, Oxford Authors (Oxford: Oxford University Press, 1987), 110.

Samuel Johnson, *Preface to the Plays of William Shakespeare* (1765), in *Works* ed. Donald Greene, Oxford Authors (Oxford: Oxford University Press, 1984), 426.

Ben Jonson, *Volpone*, in *Works*, ed. Donaldson et al. (Cambridge: Cambridge University Press, 2012) iii, 2 4 30–1

William Shakespeare, *The Comedy of Errors*, Arden2, ed. R. A. Foakes (London: Methuen, 1962). In the later quotation from Dromio of Syracuse, I use the Arden editor's 'goblins, elves, and sprites' in favour of the Oxford edition's 'goblins, oafs, and sprites' because this reading—in my view—more accurately reflects the play's mood of magic. Both the Oxford and the Arden editors feel that the original text, which reads 'goblins, owls, and sprites' must be faulty, although it too has a rather winning magical quality.

Michael Hattaway, 'The Comedies on Film' in Russell Jackson, ed., *The Cambridge Companion to Shakespeare on Film* (Cambridge: Cambridge University Press, 2000), 85–98 (86).

William Empson, *Some Versions of the Pastoral* (1935; repr. London: Chatto & Windus, 1950), 11.

George Meredith, *An Essay on Comedy* (1877; repr. London: Constable & Co, 1918), 22, 78, 87–8.

Chapter 2: Wit

Samuel Johnson, *Preface to the Plays of William Shakespeare* (1765), in *Works* ed. Donald Greene, Oxford Authors (Oxford: Oxford University Press, 1984), 429.

William Hazlitt, *Characters of Shakespeare* (1817), in *Works* ed. P. P. Howe (London: Dent, 1930), 175.

Samuel Taylor Coleridge, 'Lectures on Shakespeare', in *Works* ed. H. J. Jackson, Oxford Authors (Oxford: Oxford University Press, 1985), 641; and Samuel Taylor Coleridge, *Shakespeare Criticism*, ed. Thomas Raysor (London: Constable, 1930), 170.

William Congreve, 'Concerning Humour in Comedy', in John Dennis, *Letters upon Several Occasions* (London: Mr Dennis, 1696), 80–96 (82).

John Dryden, *Works*, ed. Keith Walker, Oxford Authors (Oxford: Oxford University Press, 1987), 111–12.

J. A. Cuddon, *A Dictionary of Literary Terms*, 2nd edition (London: Penguin, 1980).

In the quotation from Beatrice and Benedick's exchange about 'Lady Disdain' I capitalize 'Disdain' in line with William Shakespeare, *Much Ado About Nothing,* ed. Claire McEachern, Arden3 (London: Methuen, 2007) so as to emphasize her status as an abstract deity; the Oxford edition uses lowercase.

John Donne, 'Satire 2' (ll. 29–30) and 'Elegy 4' (ll. 15–16) in *Works* ed. John Carey, Oxford Authors (Oxford: Oxford University Press, 1990).

Thomas Hobbes, *Human Nature*, 2nd edition (1651), Chapter 9, 102.

Victor Raskin, *Semantic Mechanisms of Humor* (Dordrecht: D. Reide, 1985), 99.

Sigmund Freud, *Jokes and Their Relation to the Unconscious*, in *Works*, ed. James Strachey, 24 vols (London: Hogarth Press, 1953–75), vi, 232.

Chapter 3: Love

Gl'Intronati of Siena, *Gl'Ingannati*, in Bruce Penman, ed., *Five Italian Renaissance Comedies* (London: Penguin, 1978), iv.8 (p. 263).

Chapter 4: Time

Aristotle, *Poetics*, in *Classical Literary Criticism*, ed. D. A. Russell and M. Winterbottom (Oxford: Oxford University Press, 1972), 57.

Donatus, 'On Comedy' translated in O. B. Hardison Jr et al., ed., *Medieval Literary Criticism* (New York: Frederick Ungar Publishing, 1974), 47–8.

Northrop Frye, 'The Argument of Comedy', in Russ MacDonald, ed., *Shakespeare: An Anthology of Criticism and Theory 1945–2000* (Oxford: Blackwell, 2004), 93–9 (97).

Anne Barton, '*As You Like It* and *Twelfth Night*: Shakespeare's "sense of an ending"' (1972), in *Essays: Mainly Shakespearean* (Cambridge: Cambridge University Press, 1994), 91–112 (91–2).

A. D. Nuttall, *Shakespeare the Thinker* (Yale: Yale University Press, 2007).

Chapter 5: Character

Alexander Pope, 'Preface', *The Works of Shakespear*, 6 vols, 2nd edition (London, 1728).

Samuel Johnson, *Preface to the Plays of William Shakespeare* (1765), in *Works* ed. Donald Greene, Oxford Authors (Oxford: Oxford University Press, 1984), 422.

Karl Wilhelm Friedrich Schlegel, quoted in William Hazlitt, *Characters of Shakespeare* (1817), in *Complete Works*, ed. P. P. Howe (London: Dent, 1930), 174.

Edward Dowden, 'Shakspere's [*sic*] Portraiture of Women', in Edward Dowden *Transcripts and Studies* (London: Kegan Paul, 1910), 338–77 (369).

Mary Cowden Clarke, *The Girlhood of Shakespeare's Heroines in a Series of Tales*, 5 vols (Boston: Dana Estes & Col. 1891), i.vii.

Ben Jonson, *Bartholomew Fair*, in *Works*, ed. Donaldson et al. (Cambridge: Cambridge University Press, 2012), ind.11–12.

Ben Jonson, *The Alchemist*, in *Works*, ed. Donaldson et al. (Cambridge: Cambridge University Press, 2012), 2.3.49–52

E. M. Forster, *Aspects of the Novel* (1927; repr. London: Edward Arnold, 1958), 65.

Samuel Johnson, *Preface to the Plays of William Shakespeare* (1765), in *Works* ed. Donald Greene, Oxford Authors (Oxford: Oxford University Press, 1984), 427.

Henri Bergson, *Laughter: An Essay on the Meaning of Comic* [1900], trans. Cloudesley Breton and Fred Rothwell (Rockville, MA: Wildside Press, 2008).

Frederick S. Boas, *Shakspere and his Predecessors* (London: John Murray, 1896).

William W. Lawrence, *Shakespeare's Problem Comedies* (New York: Macmillan, 1931), 5.

George Whetstone, *Promos and Cassandra*, in Geoffrey Bullough, ed., *Narrative and Dramatic Sources of Shakespeare*, 8 vols (London: Routledge and Kegan Paul, 1961–1975), ii, 513.

Roger Allam in Russell Jackson and Robert Smallwood, eds, *Players of Shakespeare 3* (Cambridge: Cambridge University Press, 1993), 25–9.

Endings

Edward Dowden, *Shakspere: A Critical Study of His Mind and Art* (London: 1875; repr. Routledge, 1948), 222, vi, 36.

William Shakespeare, *Hamlet: the Texts of 1603 and 1623*, ed. Ann Thompson and Neil Taylor, Arden3 (Arden: Cengage, 2006).

Susan Snyder, *The Comic Matrix of Shakespeare's Tragedies* (Princeton, NJ: Princeton University Press, 1979), 166–7, 137.

In the case of *The Tempest* Armin's role as Trinculo is a logical deduction but in the case of Armin's playing Autolycus there is an actual eyewitness report, for which, see Simon Forman's 'Booke of Plaies', Bodleian MS Ashmole 208, fol. 202, printed in E. K. Chambers, *William Shakespeare: A Study of Facts and Problems* (Oxford: Clarendon Press, 1930), ii, 341.

William Shakespeare (attrib.), *Double Falsehood*, ed. Brean Hammond, Arden3 (London: Methuen, 2010).

Samuel Johnson, *Preface to the Plays of William Shakespeare* (1765), in *Works* ed. Donald Greene, Oxford Authors (Oxford: Oxford University Press, 1984), 425.

Further reading

C. L. Barber, *Shakespeare's Festive Comedy: A Study of Dramatic Form and its Relation to Social Custom* (Princeton: Princeton University Press, 1959).

Matthew Bevis, *Comedy: A Very Short Introduction* (Oxford: Oxford University Press, 2013).

Michael Bristol, *Carnival and Theatre: Plebeian Culture and the Structure of Authority in Renaissance England* (London: Methuen, 1985).

Keir Elam, *Shakespeare's Universe of Discourse: Language-Games in the Comedies* (Cambridge: Cambridge University Press, 1984).

Northrop Frye, 'The Argument of Comedy', *English Institute Essays 1949* (New York: Columbia University Press, 1949).

Marjorie Garber, *Vested Interests: Cross-Dressing and Cultural Anxiety* (London: Routledge, 1992).

Penny Gay, *The Cambridge Introduction to Shakespeare's Comedies* (Cambridge: Cambridge University Press, 2008).

François Laroque, *Shakespeare's Festive World: Elizabethan Seasonal Entertainment and the Professional Stage* (Cambridge: Cambridge University Press, 1991).

Alexander Leggatt, *The Cambridge Companion to Shakespearean Comedy* (Cambridge: Cambridge University Press, 2002).

Alexander Leggatt, *Shakespeare's Comedy of Love* (London: Methuen, 1974).

Michael Mangan, *A Preface to Shakespeare's Comedies* (London: Longman, 1996).

R. W. Maslen, *Shakespeare and Comedy* (London: Thompson Learning, 2006).

Robert S. Miola, *Shakespeare and Classical Comedy* (Oxford: Clarendon Press, 1994).

Ruth Nevo, *Comic Transformations in Shakespeare* (London: Methuen, 1980).

Karen Newman, *Shakespeare's Rhetoric of Comic Character: Dramatic Convention in Classical and Renaissance Comedy* (London: Methuen, 1985).

D. J. Palmer, ed., *Comedy: Developments in Criticism* (Houndmills: Palgrave, 1992).

Richard Preiss, *Clowning and Authorship in Early Modern Theatre* (Cambridge: Cambridge University Press, 2014).

Leo Salinger, *Shakespeare and the Traditions of Comedy* (Cambridge: Cambridge University Press, 1974).

Bart van Es, *Shakespeare in Company* (Oxford: Oxford University Press, 2013).

Robert Weimann, *Shakespeare and the Popular Tradition in the Theater* (Baltimore: Johns Hopkins University Press, 1978).

David Wiles, *Shakespeare's Clown: Actor and Text in the Elizabethan Playhouse* (Cambridge: Cambridge University Press, 1987).

Index

ENGLISH LITERATURE
A Very Short Introduction
Jonathan Bate

Sweeping across two millennia and every literary genre, acclaimed scholar and biographer Jonathan Bate provides a dazzling introduction to English Literature. The focus is wide, shifting from the birth of the novel and the brilliance of English comedy to the deep Englishness of landscape poetry and the ethnic diversity of Britain's Nobel literature laureates. It goes on to provide a more in-depth analysis, with close readings from an extraordinary scene in King Lear to a war poem by Carol Ann Duffy, and a series of striking examples of how literary texts change as they are transmitted from writer to reader.

www.oup.com/vsi

MEDIEVAL
LITERATURE
A Very Short Introduction
Elaine Treharne

This *Very Short Introduction* provides a compelling account of the emergence of the earliest literature in Britain and Ireland, including English, Welsh, Scottish, Irish, Anglo-Latin and Anglo-Norman. Introducing the reader to some of the greatest poetry, prose and drama ever written, Elaine Treharne discusses the historical and intellectual background to these works, and considers the physical production of the manuscripts and the earliest beginnings of print culture. Covering both well-known texts, such as *Beowulf*, *The Canterbury Tales* and the *Mabinogion*, as well as texts that are much less familiar, such as sermons, saints' lives, lyrics and histories, Treharne discusses major themes such as sin and salvation, kingship and authority, myth and the monstrous, and provides a full, but brief, account of one of the major periods in literary history.

www.oup.com/vsi

MODERN DRAMA
A Very Short Introduction
Kirsten Shepherd-Barr

The story of modern drama is a tale of extremes, testing both audiences and actors to their limits through hostility and contrarianism. Spanning 1880 to the present, Kirsten E. Shepherd-Barr shows how truly international a phenomenon modern drama has become, and how vibrant and diverse in both text and performance. This *Very Short Introduction* explores the major developments of modern drama, covering two decades per chapter, from early modernist theatre through post-war developments to more recent and contemporary theatre. Shepherd-Barr tracks the emergence of new theories from the likes of Brecht and Beckett alongside ground-breaking productions to illuminate the fascinating evolution of modern drama.

THEATRE
A Very Short Introduction
Marvin Carlson

Theatre is one of the longest-standing art forms of modern civilization. Every aspect of human activity and human culture can be, and has been, incorporated into the creation of theatre. In this *Very Short Introduction* Marvin Carlson takes a global look at how various forms of theatre-including puppetry, dance, and mime-have been interpreted and enjoyed, from Ancient Greece and Rome, to Medieval Japan and Europe, to America and beyond. Exploring the role that theatre artists play—from the actor and director to the designer and puppet-master, as well as the audience—this is an engaging exploration of what theatre has meant, and still means, to people of all ages at all times.

www.oup.com/vsi

TRAGEDY
A Very Short Introduction
Adrian Poole

What do we mean by 'tragedy' now? When we turn on the news,
does a report of the latest atrocity have any connection with
Sophocles and Shakespeare? In this *Very Short Introduction*,
Adrian Poole argues for the continuities between 'then' and 'now'.
Addressing questions about belief, blame, mourning, revenge,
pain, witnessing, timing and ending, Adrian Poole demonstrates
the age-old significance of our attempts to make sense of terrible
suffering.

www.oup.com/vsi

WILLIAM SHAKESPEARE
A Very Short Introduction
Stanley Wells

In this new offering from Stanley Wells, the pre-eminent Shakespearian scholar, comes an exploration of one of the world's greatest dramatists: William Shakespeare.

Examining Shakespeare's narrative poems, sonnets, and all of his plays, Wells outlines their sources, style, and originality over the course of Shakespeare's career, to consider the fundamental impact his work has had for subsequent generations. Written with enthusiasm and flair by a scholar who has devoted a lifetime to the study of Shakespeare and his works, this is an engaging and authoritative introduction that looks at both the world Shakespeare lived in and all of his major works, to show how and why he continues to be so influential and important to society today.

"this is an excellent place to start exploring the life and work of probably the most celebrated dramatist not only in Britain but also throughout the world." - **Shiny New Books**

com/vsi